Business Analysis

Software Testing

Usability

A Quick Guide Book
for
Better Project Management and
Faster IT Career

-Koray Yitmen-

Forewords by Rex Black, Lee Copeland, and
Dorothy Graham

ISBN: 978-605-66061-1-3

To my grandmother

Contents

Concluding Chapter

Foreword by Rex Black

Software projects are notoriously risky, especially large, complex projects. Smart professionals and managers should take steps to manage the risks associated with software projects. Ask yourself some simple, closely-related questions about your projects. If you don't know what you need to build, how can you build it? If you don't verify and validate what was built, how can you be confident it will work for the users? And, if you don't consider how the software will affect your users, why would you expect them to like it? This book helps get readers thinking about these simple—but all too often forgotten—questions.

This is a handy book for a variety of readers. I can imagine that a whole lot of project managers, product managers, business unit managers, and other IT participants and stakeholders could benefit greatly from reading this book because it would give them a better understanding of business analysis, testing, and usability. As a consultant, I have found that unrealistic expectations on the part of stakeholders are a major cause of project failure. This short, easy-to-read overview of each of these three areas should bring those stakeholders up to speed.

This book is also useful for people considering entering any of these three critical fields. Someone considering usability as a career could read the usability chapters in this book and come to a better understanding of what such a career involves. Someone considering software testing as a career could read the software testing chapters in this book and come to a better understanding of what such a career involves. Someone considering business analysis as a career could read the business analysis chapters in this book and come to a better understanding of what such a career involves.

As I noted at the start, a strong relationship exists between questions of what is to be built, whether it works, and how it affects the users. Therefore, if you are a professional tester, you will benefit from reading the chapters on business analysis and usability; I know I did. Similarly, business analysts should read the software testing and usability chapters and usability professionals should read the software testing and business analysis chapters.

Finally, since this book addresses usability, I'll close with a note on my user experience of reading this book. You'll have noticed it's short, which makes it a nice quick read. Even better, it's short because it's concise, not because it consists of entirely obvious statements. There's a lot of good content here.

And, even though there's a lot of good content in a few pages, don't think that means the book is dense and dry. It's exactly the opposite. Koray does a great job of using clever, insightful metaphors to illustrate concepts. He writes in an accessible, easy-to-read style. I have known Koray for years. While Koray is a sincere and thoughtful man, he is also a man who often wears a smile. That smile comes through as you read this book, along with the good ideas he is imparting. I hope you enjoy reading this book as much as I did.

Rex Black
President, RBCS, Inc.
Past President, ASTQB
Past President, ISTQB
Security +, CFLBA, CTFL, CMT, CTFL-AT, CTAL-FULL, CTEL-TM-FULL

Foreword by Lee Copeland

In *Business Analysis, Software Testing, Usability: A Quick Guide Book for Better Project Management and Faster IT Career*, Koray Yitmen has combined three of the most important topics in software development today. He rightly understands that if we don't create well-defined requirements (from both the users' and technicians' points of view), if we don't verify that we have built what was specified, and if we don't create a product that users find both useful and seductive, we will fail in today's marketplace. In one volume, his book addresses those three vital areas in a way that is intuitive, easy to understand, and satisfying to the reader.

I first met Koray at the TestIstanbul testing conference. As president of the ISTQB Turkish Testing Board, he organizes this marvelous and highly successful regional testing conference. Koray's substantial knowledge and experience in requirements, testing, and user experience design make him uniquely qualified to write on these three topics.

In his book Koray uses two phrases again and again. The first is "Quality is not tested, but built." This saying is decades old, but many organizations today are either ignorant of its truth or attempt to ignore it. Koray reminds us that quality is not something added at the end of product creation like spreading frosting on a cake; it must be a part of the creation process from the very beginning. Organizations that build quality products from inception are able to dedicate their resources to innovating their next opportunities. Those that build poor quality products must use their resources responding to unhappy customers and repairing defective products. While the correct choice seems obvious, many don't get it. Koray points the way.

The other phrase Koray uses is "... should first be handled as a people issue rather than a technology issue." In this wisdom, he paraphrases Gerald Weinberg's Second Law of Consulting: "No matter how it looks at first, it's always a people problem." People— their needs, wants, desires, and relationships—are the foundational elements of identifying clear requirements, precise implementation, and devoted use. Surgeons often see "cutting" as the solution to many medical problems, while internists see "medicine" as the solution to those same problems. We, as technologists, often see "technology" as the solution to technology problems. This approach is evident from the first stirrings of Agile (write code to implement those tests) and is repeated in today's DevOps (write code to implement those environments). Instead of solving a problem with more code, Koray warns us to look toward the people issues first.

To those in the IT world who need an understanding of these principles, I recommend this book.

Lee Copeland
TechWell Corporation
April 2016

Foreword by Dorothy Graham

There are many books about topics and disciplines in Information Technology. But most books concentrate on a single area. This Quick Guide by Koray Yitmen is an exception - it looks at three disciplines and ties them together. Each area informs the others, and this is an excellent idea - all benefit from cross-disciplinary insights.

With this high-level "bird's-eye view", there is still enough detail to gain an understanding of all three disciplines: Business Analysis, Software Testing and Usability. If you don't know about any of these, this book will give you an introduction to all of them; if you know one or two of them, this book will introduce you to the other(s).

The Business Analysis section starts each chapter with a short but challenging question. Think about what your answer would be before you read the chapter. Koray's answers, even if you didn't agree initially, are well-argued and make good sense. The use of business scenarios brings the points to life with realistic conversations and situations.

The section on Software Testing uses a number of interesting analogies, including road traffic and high jumping. There are fundamental descriptions of testing, including risk, coverage and the use of a basic technique.

The Usability section makes the very important distinction between Usability and User Experience (again using interesting analogies and examples). The chapter questions are not as succinct as in the first section, but there are many useful points made, especially about usability myths.

Reading this book will give you a good overview of these three disciplines, all of them critically important in IT. Congratulations to Koray for putting this book together, and also for his generosity in donating profits to schools.

Dorothy Graham, May 2016
Consultant, speaker and author

Preface

This book describes the main building blocks of business analysis, software testing, and usability disciplines. A better understanding of these three disciplines and their interactions with each other will help any professional deliver better, faster IT projects. This book is not a comprehensive guide to business analysis, software testing, or usability disciplines; rather, it is a quick guide. Throughout the book, different perspectives are brought to the following interesting comparisons and relationships:

Business Analysis
- Business analysts and software testers
- Usability specialists and business analysts
- System analysts and business analysts
- Project management and business analysis
- Business requirements and system requirements
- Use cases and user requirements
- The object-oriented approach versus the business process approach
- Functional requirements and non-functional requirements
- Activity diagrams versus flowcharts
- Scope management and stakeholder management
- Change management and project management
- Process flows, class diagrams, and sequence diagrams
- Use case modelling and project scope definition
- In-scope items and out-of-scope items
- Unclear requirements and test cases
- Traceability matrix and gold plating
- Change request management process and requirements management tools
- Impact analysis and traceability matrix
- Project Management Institute (PMI) knowledge areas and business analysis

Software Testing
- Software test design techniques and high jump techniques
- Software testing and road traffic
- Priority versus severity
- Risk and software testing
- Software testing levels and software testing types

- The MoSCoW prioritization technique and the software test design technique
- Black-box testing versus white-box testing
- Statement coverage versus decision coverage

Usability
- UX and usability
- Usability specialists and business analysts
- Usability testing versus user acceptance testing
- Interaction design and process flow design
- User profiling versus persona identification

Who Is This Book for?
This book is for anyone who wants to have a high-level overview of the three disciplines needed to deliver better, faster IT projects: business analysis, software testing and usability, and how they fit together. This book will also help experienced professionals stimulate conversations and debates about the topics and concepts mentioned in its chapters.

In addition to helping professionals deliver better, faster IT projects, this book will also help the future of our world—our children. One hundred percent of the net profit from this book's sales will be donated towards primary school initiatives.

How to Read This Book
Although all chapters complement each other, each chapter can be read separately based on its related discipline: business analysis, software testing, or usability. For this purpose, the chapter breakdown is as follows:
- Business Analysis chapters: 1-5
- Software Testing chapters: 6-10
- Usability chapters: 11-14

Chapter 15 investigates the tendency to place blame for failed IT projects.

Each chapter starts with a challenging question. In order to enhance your learning experience, try to answer the chapter question before reading the chapter. For your questions, comments, and suggestions, you can contact the author via email at koray.yitmen@keytorc.com.

Acknowledgements

I would like to thank the following people (in alphabetical order) for reviewing the drafts of this book: Anna McMurray, Barış Sarıalioğlu, Berk Dülger, Besim Kosova, Bora Sıpal, Burcu Nurcan, Canberk Akduygu, Dorothy Graham, Emrah Yayıcı, Emre Yayıcı, Esra Eş, İsmail Dağgeçen, Lee Copeland, Mehmet Yitmen, Merve İçöz, Pelin Başkan, Pınar Cinali, Rex Black, Sera Seren Dizen, and Şenay Yitmen.

About the Author

As a father, philanthropist, consultant, instructor, and business partner, Koray Yitmen has led many multi-national, cross-functional teams in the banking, telecommunications, insurance, media, and information technology (IT) industries for more than 15 years. Challenged by the diversity of his projects' cultural, domain, and people issues, Koray has succeeded by putting the needs of his projects' target users first. In 2000, he started his career as a technology consultant at Accenture (formerly Arthur Andersen). Having worked at Accenture, he has been the business partner of Keytorc Software Testing Services, BA-Works Business Analysis Services, and UXservices UX Design Company since 2005. He has a B.S. in Computer Science from Middle East Technical University, Ankara and an MBA in Entrepreneurship from Babson College, MA. He is the board member of the International Institute of Business Analysis (IIBA®) Istanbul Chapter, the president of Turkish Testing Board — a member of the International Software Testing Qualifications Board (ISTQB®), the president of User Experience Professionals' Association (UXPA) Istanbul Chapter, and the chair of TestIstanbul software testing conferences. He is a strong advocate of the business motto "Quality is not tested, but built" and tries to implement this motto in every IT project in which he is involved. His greatest happiness of life is giving back to the community.

Business Analysis
Chapters

Chapter 1

Business Requirements, User Requirements, and Functional Requirements

Question
Assume that one is working as a business analyst in a mobile banking application development project and is using the terms below to organize business analysis deliverables.

How should the following terms be sorted from the most generic to the most specific? (Most generic 1   2 3   4 5   Most specific)
- ___ User requirements
- ___ Objectives
- ___ Business requirements
- ___ Functional requirements
- ___ Non-functional requirements

Business Requirements, User Requirements, and Functional Requirements

The terms introduced in the chapter question might be heard in conversations among project team members of a mobile application development project. The following is the CEO's speech during the project's kick-off meeting:

CEO:

Dear Colleagues,

We are on the eve of a breakthrough change in the usage patterns of banking customers. For the last five years, we have been experiencing a huge shift in transaction volumes from traditional banking to online banking. Now, with the widespread use of smart phones, mobile banking is on the horizon. In order to keep up with the mobile banking trend and even to become one of the trendsetters in this new medium, we must act fast and set de facto standards with the help of our mobile applications. In addition, our mobile banking applications will help us not only reduce our operational costs but also increase our efficiency and effectiveness.

With these goals in mind, we are gathered today for the kick-off meeting of our first mobile banking application development project. Let us never forget that mobile banking requires a paradigm shift in our mindsets. For example, as opposed to a typical customer, we now have to imagine a new type of customer who may never stop by our branch; the only thing a customer now needs is a mobile banking app. We must recognize that mobile technology is more than a new channel; it is a disruptive force in customer behavior. Consequently, we must be prepared for the challenges that the mobile banking brings.

I wish you good luck and a successful project.

Because the CEO addressed the big picture and the major motivations behind the project, let us start by pinpointing the most general concepts throughout the speech, such as objectives and business requirements which are numbers 1 and 2:

Objectives

"In order to keep up with the mobile banking trend and even to become one of the trendsetters in this new medium, we must act fast and set de facto standards with the help of our mobile applications. In addition, our mobile banking applications will help us not only reduce our operational costs but also increase our efficiency and effectiveness."

Here, the CEO has pointed out two objectives: the first is a very general one—her bank's intention to take part in the mobile world and even lead it—the other is more specific—reducing costs and increasing the efficiency and effectiveness of the bank's operations. These two objectives serve as the guidelines for all efforts and decisions made during the project.

Business Requirements

"Our First Mobile Banking Application Development Project"

In order to achieve the two objectives that the CEO mentioned, a specific activity or a project must be addressed. In the CEO's kick-off speech, the project to be implemented to achieve the objectives is introduced as Our First Mobile Banking Application Development Project. In business analysis terminology, the name of the project and its short description is called the business requirement.

Having identified the business requirement, let us examine the details. Assume that as a business analyst, in order to elaborate the business requirement, one must conduct requirements elicitation sessions by using various elicitation techniques such as brainstorming, focus groups, interviews, and requirements workshops. During these sessions, one might participate in conversations similar to the following one:

Business Analyst: *Who is your target customer segment for this mobile app?*

Business Unit: *Well, we are aiming at time-poor customers who have no time for banking during their daily hassle. They complete their*

6

banking transactions while on the way home, perhaps on the train or bus, or even in the car. So the app should be very fast and easy to use.

Business Analyst: *From your customer description, I understand that rather than having a demographic segmentation based on age, marital status, or monthly salary, you want to segment and target your users based on their usage of banking services. Am I right?*

Business Unit: *Definitely, user behavior is much more important than numbers and statistics. Our time-poor customers may be young adults, or they may be in their 30s, 40s, 50s, or even 70s. Customers whose time is scarce and valuable are on our target list.*

Business Analyst: *Fine. So, what would these kinds of customers expect from the mobile app?*

Business Unit: *Since mobile banking is a very new medium, and we are targeting a wide spectrum of customers, we want to keep the app simple and include only basic banking features such as checking balances, making transfers, and paying bills.*

In the conversation above, the business unit's statement that *"We want to include basic banking features such as checking balances, making transfers, and paying bills"* clearly describes the mobile banking users' needs, which are called "user requirements" and they are number 3 on the list. Those needs can be easily modeled by using the use case technique, as shown in the following:

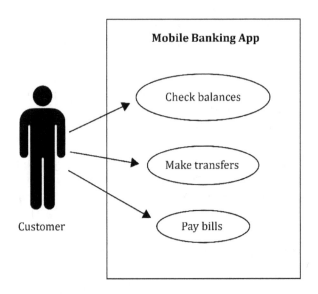

Figure 1.1 Use case model of mobile banking application

By defining user requirements, the business requirement is elaborated on, and the project scope is defined. To sum up, user requirements are check balances, make transfers and pay bills.

But simply listing user requirements does not ensure successful implementation of the mobile app. Software developers need more detail. For each user requirement defined, business analysts should also examine the steps users should follow. In business analysis terminology, these are called functional requirements and are number 4 on the list. For example:

Business Analyst: *What steps should users follow while making transfers?*

Business Unit: *Based on our user surveys and our experience in online banking, the most efficient way for our users to make transfers is as follows:*

Functional Requirements for the "Making Transfers" User Requirement

FR1.	User selects the debit account
FR2.	User enters the credit account
FR3.	User enters the amount to be transferred
FR4.	User selects the date
FR5.	Users clicks the 'Send' button

In the above flow of events, the primary scenario for the "making transfers" user requirement is described. Since a primary scenario captures normal behavior and excludes exceptions, specific cases, and extensions, this scenario only includes the basic flow of activities when a user uses the system based on the user requirement. Exceptions, specific cases, and extensions may be expressed using secondary scenarios. For example, if a user wanted to enter the amount first, then date, then the accounts.

Non-Functional Requirements for the "Making Transfers" User Requirement

In order to complement the functional requirements, non-functional requirements should be defined. Non-functional requirements are number 5 among the terms introduced in the chapter question. In the following conversation, the business unit describes one of the non-functional requirements:

Business Analyst: *While making money transfers, does the user need special requirements in terms of usability, performance, or security?*

Business Unit: *Well, since we are targeting a wide spectrum of users, we are expecting to receive a peak load of one thousand concurrent users. The system should be able to handle one thousand concurrent users during peak times.*

The non-functional requirement that *"one thousand concurrent users should be handled during peak times"* is a performance requirement of the "making transfers" user requirement. If the business unit is further questioned, more non-functional requirements could most likely be gathered and vague terms such as "handled" can be further defined.

Below, the terms from the chapter question are ordered from most generic to most specific:
1. Objective: the starting point of the project.
2. Business requirement: the brief summary of the project.
3. User requirements: the scope of the project.
4. Functional requirements: the steps (from the users' perspective) that constitute the user requirements.
5. Non-functional requirements: the requirements that complement a functional requirement.

The relationship between each term is shown below:

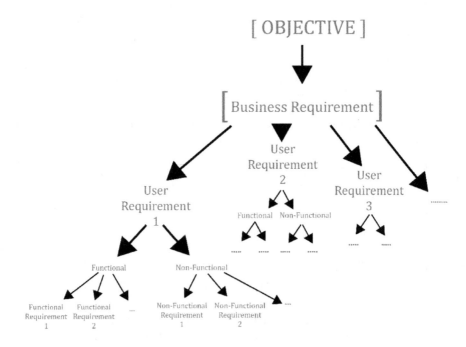

Figure 1.2 The relationship map of objective and different kinds of requirement

A business analyst may wonder where the constraints and the assumptions fit in the above relationship map. However, because they can affect any one of the above terms, such constraints and assumptions may exist at any level.

Constraints

Constraints are the limitations that may affect the objective, business requirements, user requirements, functional requirements, and non-functional requirements of the project. For example, as the CEO stated during her speech, *"Now, with the widespread use of smart phones, mobile banking is on the horizon"* is a constraint stating that the smart phone penetration rate is the most important factor to the growth of mobile banking. This constraint will affect the penetration of the mobile banking app into the customer base, affecting the project's objective of reducing operational costs, which means that the lower the smart phone penetration rate is, the lower the return on the investment of the mobile application development project will be.

Compared to the high level constraint of smart phone penetration rate affecting the project, a constraint related to one of the user requirements will only affect the process flow of that requirement. For example, a constraint given by a business unit stating that a customer must have a positive account balance in order to make a money transfer will only affect the "making transfers" user requirement.

Assumptions

Similar to constraints, assumptions may also affect the objective, the business requirement, user requirements, functional requirements, and non-functional requirements of the project. In definition, an assumption is a forecast: a thing that is accepted as true or as certain to happen, without proof. For example, the CEO's assumption that mobile banking requires a major change in the way one thinks about the typical customer may affect many user requirements of mobile banking, especially user requirements which require the customer's physical presence at the branch, such as the signing of a document. The process flows of these kinds of user requirements should be designed according to this assumption.

On the other hand, the business unit's assumption that the system will accommodate a peak load of a thousand concurrent users for making transfers will only affect the non-functional requirement of the "making transfers" user requirement.

The final order and the structure of the terms are as follows:

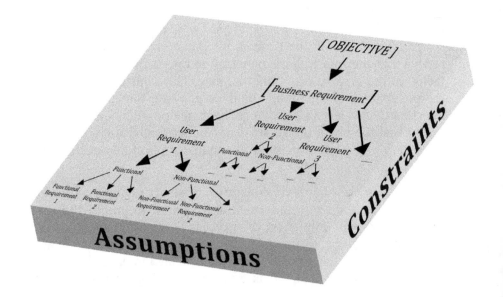

Chapter 2

How, What, Why, and Who: What Is Their Order of Importance?

Question
Assume that one is working as a business analyst on an IT project. Included in the requirements elicitation sessions, is the set of questions below used to identify users' needs. Rank the questions according to their order of importance (from the user's point of view). (Highest priority 1, lowest priority 4)

- __ How?
- __ What?
- __ Why?
- __ Who?

How, What, Why, and Who: What Is Their Order of Importance?

In order to illustrate the difficulty of asking the right questions to identify users and their needs, the following example from the air delivery and freight services industry will be analyzed. Imagine the following conversation between a walk-in customer and a company representative working at one of the companies operating in this industry. The conversation is taking place in an office located in New York City:

Company representative: Good morning, how may I help you?

Customer: Hi, I want this package to be shipped to Washington University in St. Louis.

Company representative: Sure, what are the contents of the package, and when would you like it delivered?

Customer: Well, it is a small package, its weight may be around one pound, and I want it to be delivered in at most four days. But there are fragile articles in it, and they must be delivered undamaged.

Company representative: No worries. It will be there on time without any hassle.

Customer: Thank you.

WHO?

By asking "how may I help you?", the company representative tries to identify whether or not this person is a potential customer, as walk-ins are sometimes just tourists asking for directions. Having identified the potential customer, the company representative then asks the questions regarding the package delivery details.

Without first understanding whether a walk-in is a potential customer, it makes no sense to ask further questions. This is also true for IT projects. If the right users cannot be identified at the beginning of the project, the requirements gathered during the requirements elicitation sessions from the wrong users will make no sense. The term used to describe the focus on the right users and their needs is "User Centered Analysis and Design." By identifying the appropriate users, IT projects can be delivered successfully. The following case study is a concrete example of the business analyst failing to identify the appropriate user, thereby resulting in a useless product:

Assume that a project team is working on developing a laser pointer. Although sufficient user research involving potential customers has not yet been conducted, the project team concludes that an ergonomic and functional laser pointer with slide changer should be developed. After launching the product and implementing an aggressive marketing campaign, the team realizes that there is little interest in the product from the intended primary customer segment, large organizations. This drives the company to conduct thorough user research and approach the users in this segment in order to find the root cause of the failure. Here are the responses that may be heard from a prospective customer during one of the interviews:

Business Analyst: *What do you think of this laser pointer?*

Prospective Customer: *Well, it seems to be a very powerful laser pointer. I like its shape and it seems very ergonomic. It is very easy to hold in my hand and to change the slides. But I rarely give presentations for my work. So why should I pay for it? I can use the shared one in the office when I need it.*

The prospective customer is right; though the laser pointer may be very user-friendly, why should she buy it if its features are not useful for her. Consequently, it is very important to understand the user and her needs, and therefore first identify the right user, in this case independent consultants or trainers who also do conference presentations. If the right user cannot be identified, the answers supplied by the user are insignificant. Based on this reasoning, the question "Who?" appears to be the most important question.

WHAT?

An examination of the package delivery case study further illustrates how to ask the right questions to identify users' needs. The customer has stated that:

"I want this package to be shipped to Washington University in St. Louis."

Shipping a package is obviously the customer's primary need. Without understanding the customer's primary need, the company representative cannot move forward with additional questions. The customer's primary need can be identified by asking "what is the company supposed to do?" The more appropriate question in IT projects is not "what is the company supposed to do?", but "what is the system supposed to do?" In business analysis terminology, the answer given to "what is the system supposed to do?" is called a business, user or functional requirement depending on its level of detail.

WHY?

After identifying the walk-in as a potential customer and understanding her need, the company representative should then question the alignment of the customer's need with the company goals. In the package delivery case study, since the customer's need to ship a package is aligned with the company's goal of profiting from package delivery, the company representative does not feel the need to ask why the customer wants to ship the package.

The question "why?" should follow the question "what?" in IT projects, as well. During requirements elicitation sessions involving users, a business analyst should not act as a voice recorder and should not comply with all of the users' wishes. A business analyst should instead filter users' needs by questioning the purpose of each need and rejecting the needs not aligned with the project goal, prioritizing the rest according to their value added to the project goal.

For example, in a CRM project whose goal is customer retention, customer acquisition user requirements should be either rejected or ranked as low priority. Without questioning the purpose of the need, a business analyst does not understand the necessity of the need. Because users tend to include all of their needs within the scope of the project, questioning the purpose of the need will act as a filter and keep the project on the track.

HOW?

Once the company representative in the package delivery case study has identified the potential customer, understood the customer's need, and validated the need's alignment with the company's objective, he/she should then think of ways in which to deliver the package within its given constraints. For example:

- Should the package be loaded onto the truck leaving for Washington University tomorrow?
- If tomorrow's truck is full, should the package be loaded onto the next truck, assuming there is enough time for delivery?
- Should the package be shipped via air delivery?
- Or, if a four-day delivery time is acceptable, should the package be loaded onto tomorrow's Washington University-bound freight train?

From the sequence of questions asked during the conversation between the company representative and the customer, it is obvious that "what?" should precede "how?" In IT projects, the corresponding question to "how?" is "How does the system do what it is supposed to do?", which is called the system requirement in business analysis terminology.

The importance of the order of the questions asked by the company representative can be further illustrated from the following conversation in the package delivery case study:

Assume that when the walk-in customer enters the office, the company representative is busy assisting other customers and answering phone calls. While the customer is stating the address to which she wants the package delivered, the company representative misses the words "St. Louis." By chance, there is another "Washington University," but very far away from St. Louis. It is Central Washington University, located in Ellensburg, Washington. In a confident voice, the company representative confirms the delivery of the package and recommends an express delivery campaign at the same price as regular delivery.

Figure 2.1 Washington University in St. Louis vs Central Washington University

Unfortunately, the company representative has not only misunderstood the address but has also promised an even faster service without any extra fees. Unsurprisingly, the package will be delivered to the wrong address, and the customer will likely soon be searching for her package. She may even phone the call center and complain about the company on social media, a true disaster.

In such a case, although the company seems to provide superior customer service by providing express delivery at no additional cost, the service provided has no value, since the company representative did not properly understand the customer's need. In IT projects, it may seem impossible that one could make such a huge mistake, but it happens, especially when project team members are directly interacting with users. Project team members aim to quickly solve the problem, focusing on the system side of the solution without first properly understanding the user's need. For example, while listening to the user and her need, a business analyst may prematurely shift her focus from actually listening to the user to finding a solution (details such as which service to call in the application layer, which database table to query, or which part of the code to modify). In short, by focusing on the solution, the business analyst may actually neglect the user and her need. Business analysts with software development backgrounds often fall into this trap. So what should business analysts do? Business analysts should focus on "what?" and without well understanding and validating it, should not move to "how?" In the package delivery case study, truck delivery, train delivery, and air delivery all relate to "how?"

But what about the other constraints mentioned by the customer at the beginning of the conversation, such as the four-day delivery requirement and the fragile contents? Don't those constraints constitute the *"how?"* as well? In actuality, these constraints relate instead to how the system should work. In business analysis terminology, these constraints are called "non-functional requirements", which complement the functional requirements such as in terms of usability, performance, security, reliability and compatibility.

To sum up, in order to conduct a successful business analysis, a business analyst must find the correct answers to the following questions in the given order:
1. "Who?": Who is the appropriate user?
2. "What?" (the business, the user or the functional requirement): What is the system supposed to do?
3. "Why?" (the objective): Why does the user need what the system offers, and are the user's needs aligned with the project goal?
4. "How?" (the non-functional requirement): How should the system work?

It is the system analyst's responsibility to identify system requirements (how the system does what it is supposed to do). In the case of the absence of a system analyst on a project team, the responsibility of finding the answer to this question then shifts from the system analyst to the business analyst.

Chapter 3

The Business Process Approach Versus the Object-Oriented Approach

Question

What is the main logical difference between the business process approach and the object-oriented approach to developing software?

    a. Their approach to functional requirements
    b. Their approach to non-functional requirements
    c. Their approach to system requirements
    d. Their approach to user requirements
    e. There is no difference

The Business Process Approach Versus the Object-Oriented Approach

Both the business process approach and the object-oriented approach are methodologies used to understand the context of the business problem or opportunity. In a business process approach the system is viewed as a collection of processes where data and processes are handled separately. Flowchart, workflow, and entity-relationship diagrams are the most common diagramming types used in this approach. In the object-oriented approach the system is viewed as a collection of objects where data and processes are handled together. Use case, activity, and class diagrams are the most common diagramming types used in this approach.

The following ATM case study will outline the main differences between the business process approach and the object-oriented approach.

In this case study, which describes the analysis and design of an ATM, the requirements listed below are modeled by using both the business process and object-oriented approaches:
- Business Requirement
- User Requirements
- Functional Requirements
- System Requirements

Business Requirement

In both approaches, the business requirement can be defined as follows:

To provide automated banking services to customers without the customer having to make a trip to the bank.

User Requirements

User requirements are modeled as follows in both approaches:

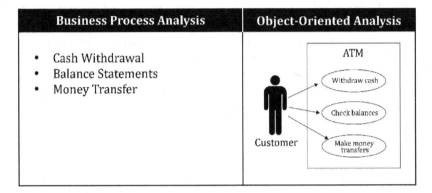

Business Process Analysis	Object-Oriented Analysis

Figure 3.1 Modeling user requirements in business process analysis and object-oriented analysis

As seen in the table above, while use case diagrams are used in object-oriented analysis, simple language is used to describe the user requirements in business process analysis. Another difference between the two approaches is that the object-oriented approach is more user-centric. For instance, in object-oriented analysis, "withdraw cash" is used instead of "cash withdrawal". Those two differences might be thought as the main differences between the business process approach and the object-oriented approach, but they are not; they are only the symbolic differences between the two approaches.

Functional Requirements

In the following pages, the "cash withdrawal" user requirement will be analyzed in order to show the difference between business process analysis and object-oriented analysis in terms of functional requirements. Functional requirements are the steps to be executed in order to achieve a specific goal. While business process analysis uses flowcharts to model the functional requirements, object-oriented analysis uses activity diagrams, as shown in the following:

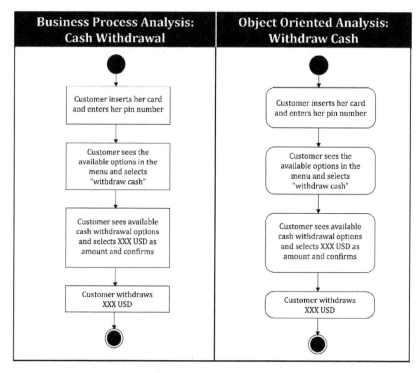

Business Process Analysis: Cash Withdrawal	Object Oriented Analysis: Withdraw Cash
Customer inserts her card and enters her pin number	Customer inserts her card and enters her pin number
Customer sees the available options in the menu and selects "withdraw cash"	Customer sees the available options in the menu and selects "withdraw cash"
Customer sees available cash withdrawal options and selects XXX USD as amount and confirms	Customer sees available cash withdrawal options and selects XXX USD as amount and confirms
Customer withdraws XXX USD	Customer withdraws XXX USD

Figure 3.2 Modeling functional requirements in business process analysis and object-oriented analysis

So far, both approaches seem almost identical, except for the minor differences between the symbols used (e.g., while the functional requirement is represented by a rectangle in the business process approach, a rounded rectangle is used in the object-oriented approach).

System Requirements

While designing system requirements, the focus should be shifted from what the system is supposed to do to how the system does what it is supposed to do, indicating a shift from the analysis phase to the design phase. The following examples show how analysis and design are integrated in each approach:

Business Process Analysis and Design

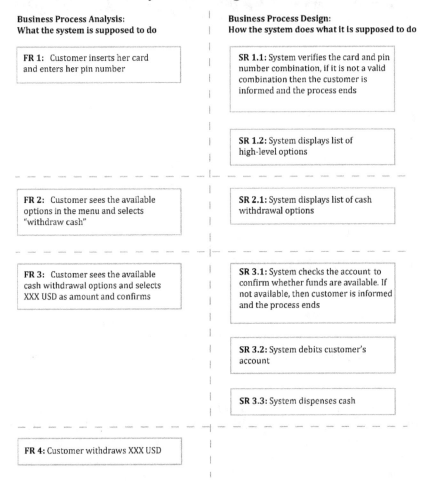

Business Process Analysis:
What the system is supposed to do

FR 1: Customer inserts her card and enters her pin number

FR 2: Customer sees the available options in the menu and selects "withdraw cash"

FR 3: Customer sees the available cash withdrawal options and selects XXX USD as amount and confirms

FR 4: Customer withdraws XXX USD

Business Process Design:
How the system does what it is supposed to do

SR 1.1: System verifies the card and pin number combination, if it is not a valid combination then the customer is informed and the process ends

SR 1.2: System displays list of high-level options

SR 2.1: System displays list of cash withdrawal options

SR 3.1: System checks the account to confirm whether funds are available. If not available, then customer is informed and the process ends

SR 3.2: System debits customer's account

SR 3.3: System dispenses cash

Figure 3.3 Business process analysis and design

As shown in the above table, in business process analysis and design, there are one or more corresponding system actions for each user action. Those system actions are then converted into system functions, and then recursively decomposed into sub-functions until simple elements that can be directly represented using programming languages are obtained. See the following functional decomposition as an example:

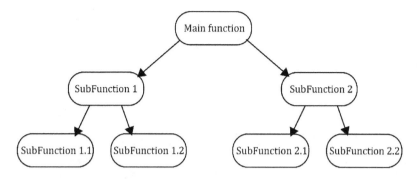

Figure 3.4 Functional decomposition of system actions in business process design

Object-Oriented Design

Contrary to business process design, object-oriented design views the system as a collection of objects. In the object-oriented design approach, functions are represented as types of collaborations between the objects that comprise the system as shown in the following example design of a simple car system.

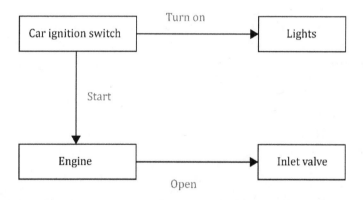

Figure 3.5 Modeling of a car system in object-oriented design

In the object-oriented approach, objects are built from classes. A class is an abstraction that statically captures the behavior of objects. A class describes the state of objects in terms of attributes (data members), and behavior in terms of methods (functions and procedures). A class can be regarded as the DNA of the corresponding object. Different from the business process design approach, the object-oriented design approach handles data and functions together in one class.

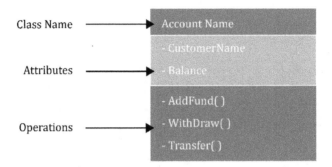

Figure 3.6 Class diagram example

Since the object-oriented approach models the design by using objects instead of functions, the modeling of the design is completely different from that of the business process approach.

Object-Oriented Analysis and Design

The ATM case study further illustrates how design is integrated with analysis in an object-oriented approach. Assume that for the cash withdrawal user requirement, the system requires the classes below in order to implement customer actions:
- ATM
- Bank
- Account
- Customer

By using the above classes, the system can be designed and integrated with analysis as follows:

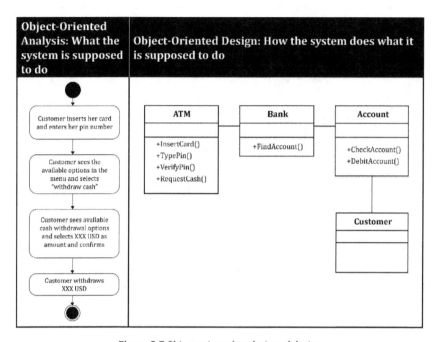

Object-Oriented Analysis: What the system is supposed to do	Object-Oriented Design: How the system does what it is supposed to do

Figure 3.7 Object-oriented analysis and design

As seen from the above model, it is not very clear how the integration between analysis and design is achieved. The answer lies within another diagram (called a sequence diagram) of the object-oriented approach. Sequence diagrams are temporal representations of objects and their interactions to describe one path (scenario) through a use case. Sequence diagrams establish the connection between the process flow and the objects — thus, the connection between analysis and design. For example, the sequence diagram for the cash withdrawal user requirement is as follows:

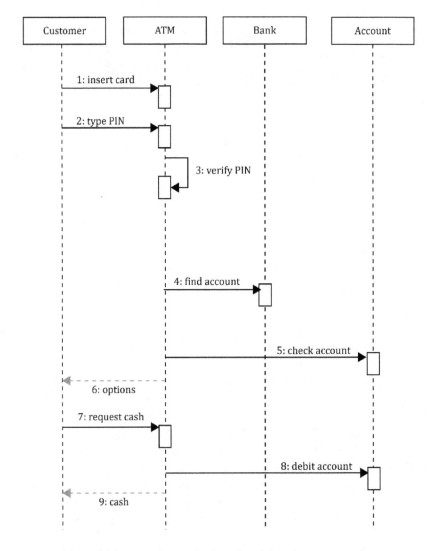

Figure 3.8 Sequence diagram for the cash withdrawal user requirement

The sequence diagram, clearly illustrates the integration of process flow with objects, as well as the integration of analysis and design.

To conclude, the main difference between the business process approach and the object-oriented approach is their approach to the system requirements and thus design.

Chapter 4

Project Management and Business Analysts

Question

In the fifth edition of *Project Management Body of Knowledge (PMBOK®)*, the Project Management Institute (PMI) defines ten project management knowledge areas.

Which *two* of the project management knowledge areas below are most related to business analysts?

a. Integration Management
b. Scope Management
c. Time Management
d. Cost Management
e. Quality Management
f. Human Resource Management
g. Communication Management
h. Risk Management
i. Procurement Management
j. Stakeholder Management

Project Management and Business Analysts

According to PMI, a project is defined as

"a temporary endeavor undertaken to create a unique product or service." [PMBOK® 5th Edition]

But creating a unique product or service on time and within budget constraints does not guarantee a success. Why? The answer lies in the requirements. Although the project team may have delivered the requirements within the given constraints, the requirements delivered might not be the right ones. Therefore, based on poorly defined requirements, the project team may deliver a product or service misaligned with users' needs and expectations. A close examination of a simple case study will solidify this assertion:

A carpenter is working rigorously on several chairs a customer has ordered. He finishes and delivers them on time but is shocked when the customer exclaims, "we do not need any extra chairs, what we need is a round dinner table. Probably you confused the orders!" In this case, the customer is correct. Although the chairs the carpenter delivered were in perfect condition and ergonomically designed, they did not please the customer. The project has failed. The take-away from the carpenter case study can be formalized by first doing the right thing then doing it right. This means that project quality is first dependent on how well the requirements are defined, and then by how well they are translated into a product or service.

It can be easily inferred from the above case study that the success of a project is in the hands of customers and their requirements. Since managing requirements is the main responsibility of business analysts, the answer to the chapter question, then, is that the two key factors (customers and requirements) of a successful IT project correlate to their broader PMI knowledge area counterparts—stakeholder management and scope management. Consequently, sharpening their skills in these two knowledge areas will help business analysts ensure their project's success.

A business analyst may wonder about the remaining eight PMI knowledge areas. These are the constraints that must be managed well in order to successfully deliver the requirements to stakeholders. The remaining eight PMI knowledge areas complement the stakeholder and scope management knowledge areas.

While managing stakeholders and scope, business analysts will face many challenges. The following are the most useful how-to strategies used to overcome these challenges:

Challenge 1: How to manage out-of-scope change requests/demands

Although out-of-scope change requests/demands are very common in many IT projects, bad management of them constitutes one of the main threats to successful scope management— thus, to successful project management. Out-of-scope change requests/demands can slowly change the course of a project. An analogy between scope management and the organization of a family picnic will illustrate how out-of-scope change requests/demands destroy IT projects:

Assume that a Sunday family picnic has been organized. The picnic basket is ready, arrangements have been made, and family members have gathered at the house to leave for the picnic on Sunday morning. On the way to the picnic area, a nephew begins talking about a newly-opened amusement park located on the way to the picnic area and suggests stopping by to spend some discount coupons. Why not? The family drives to the amusement park, and all the family members enjoy themselves for a few hours. After the amusement park, everyone is ready to go the picnic. However, on the way to the picnic area, the family passes a large billboard advertising a huge discount on HD TVs at one of the popular electronic stores. Since the family enjoys watching TV, they can't help but stop by. After two hours, the family is carrying a brand new HD TV to the van. A perfect deal!

The day has been perfect, and everyone has had fun. The family has bought a brand new TV, but something is missing; it is the picnic they were planning to have. In the end, there was no time left for the picnic; it was forgotten and ignored. The same is true for IT projects. IT projects all begin with an objective in mind, but unfortunately, with out-of-scope change requests/demands, the course of the project changes, leading to a very different project in the end. For example, the course of a customer relationship management (CRM) project with a customer retention objective may be altered by a demand of a CRM module targeting customer acquisition. Although acquiring customers is attractive and adds value to the company, this out-of-scope demand will alter the project's course, just as in the picnic analogy. These kinds of out-of-scope demands must be rejected in order to secure the scope of the project and keep it on its initially-defined course. In order to secure these goals, the following measures should be taken:

- First, set a clear project objective. Ensure that the objective is clearly communicated to all stakeholders. Abide by the objective throughout the project, and evaluate change requests/demands accordingly.
- At the beginning of the project, list not only "in-scope" items, but also "out-of-scope" items. This will help the business analyst clarify the boundaries of the scope to project members.
- Define change request/demand management processes. Handle every change request/demand accordingly, and do not allow anyone to bypass the process.

Challenge 2: How to establish common business analysis terminology among project team members and define better requirements

Although business analysts may assume that they have clearly defined the project scope and requirements, other project team members (e.g., system analysts, software developers, software testers, and enterprise architects) might be unable to understand and implement these requirements. The most common reasons behind this conflict may be addressed as follows:

Reason 1: Uncategorized requirements

Solution 1: Uncategorized requirements create confusion among project team members and leave room for mistakes. Requirements should therefore be categorized. According to the most general classification scheme, business, user, functional, non-functional, and system requirement types may be used to categorize requirements.

Reason 2: User interface (UI) designs are regarded as requirements

Solution 2: Since UI designs serve as snapshots of requirements, it is difficult for other project team members to see the big picture. Process flows should first be defined, and then UIs should be designed based on these flows.

Reason 3: Only functional requirements are defined

Solution 3: Non-functional requirements should also be defined. Non-functional requirements are the complements of functional requirements and operate similarly to the way in which adjectives precede nouns (e.g., red apple; where noun "apple" can be considered a functional requirement, and adjective "red" can be considered a non-functional requirement). Without the adjective, meaning is incomplete. This is true for requirements as well.

Challenge 3: How to identify all project stakeholders

The project is on track; every requirement has been delivered on time and within given constraints, but just before the project's release, one of the business units (for example, the law department) raises a major concern, claiming that the product/project is not what they wanted. The law department may go even further and assert that the project violates the law. This may come as a surprise to the project team, but similar cases often happen. The following are the potential reasons behind such cases:

Reasons: In some cases, stakeholder identification is not properly conducted, leading to missing stakeholders. In other cases, although stakeholder identification may be properly conducted, and stakeholders may be accurately identified, only the proxies' needs (such as business units or their representatives) have been met (rather than the needs of the real stakeholders), due to lack of time and budget constraints. This approach leads to discrepancies between real needs and the requirements gathered. For instance, in a mobile banking application development project, consulting only with bank employees to identify the end users' needs will result in missing requirements and misunderstandings in the requirements that are gathered.

Solution: Different user groups should be identified and invited to participate in the requirements elicitation sessions. During these sessions, different requirements elicitation techniques–ranging from brainstorming, focus groups, interviews, and requirements workshops–which are most suitable for the session objective and users should be used. However, business analysts should not be limited to only these techniques but should conduct field research and observe users in their natural environments.

Challenge 4: How to prevent unclear requirements

Examples of unclear requirements:

Requirement 1: *The core banking system should process transactions quickly.*

How quickly should transactions be processed? What is the definition of quickly? Is it 1 minute, 1 second, or 1 millisecond?

Requirement 2: *User interfaces should be user friendly.*

What is the definition of user friendly? And for whom should user interfaces be user friendly? For children, teenagers, or seniors?

These kinds of unclear requirements are difficult to comprehend and can lead to errors in implementation.

Solution: Although unclear requirements are the main problems in business analysis documents, they are easy to identify. In order to verify whether a requirement is clear, a test case should be written based on that requirement. If a test case cannot be written easily based on the requirement, then the requirement is most likely an unclear requirement and must be revised. For example, when test cases are written for Requirement 1 and Requirement 2, the difficulty of identifying the expected results of each requirement becomes clear.

Challenge 5: How to prioritize requirements

Well-defined and structured requirements do not guarantee a successful project. Unless other project team members are aware of the relative importance of the requirements, they will be confused about where to begin. Project team members will most probably begin with the simplest or most interesting requirements, neither of is an appropriate approach.

Solution: This challenge can only be overcome by aligning the priorities of the requirements with the priorities of the project and the users. The most common and easiest technique to prioritize requirements is to classify them as high, medium and low, but a more detailed technique such as MoSCoW (must, should, could, won't) or Radar charts can be used. The accuracy of the prioritization depends entirely on how well the project objective and the user priorities are identified.

Challenge 6: How to overcome gold plating

Gold plating is the addition of any feature not considered in the original scope plan [PMBOK®]. Since gold plating is beyond the level deemed by the customer as being sufficient, it has no value and only adds complications to the project; thus, it should be avoided.

Solution: A traceability matrix should be used to link every business requirement with user requirements, every user requirement with functional requirements, every user requirement with test cases, every functional requirement with code, every code with test cases, and test cases with bugs. By establishing such links, not only among requirements but also between requirements and work products, traceability will be achieved, which will prevent any functionality from appearing in the scope without first being officially verified.

Challenge 7: How to handle change requests

Business analysts may often not be aware of the effect personal relationships have on change requests. While a stakeholder having a strong relationship with project team members could convince project team members to add a low priority or out-of-scope change request to the project scope, another stakeholder with a weak relationship might not be able to convince project team members to add an urgent and high priority change request.

Solution: In order to overcome this challenge, a change request management process should be defined and then supported by implementing requirements management tools.

Challenge 8: How to manage impact analysis

Stakeholders may mistakenly believe that all change requests are urgent and hold the highest priority.

Solution: There should be an impact analysis process in which each change request is evaluated objectively according to some predefined criteria. Having a traceability matrix is a prerequisite for a well-functioning impact analysis process.

To sum up, if business analysts pay close attention to the above eight "how-tos," they will be able to manage the project scope and project stakeholders more efficiently and effectively, leading to more successful projects.

Chapter 5

Employees, Technology, and Resistance to Change

Question
How should resistance to change be confronted during an internal IT project?

a. By conducting visioning and informative workshops
b. By offering training to resistant employees
c. By applying work-shadowing techniques to transfer knowledge among employees
d. By demonstrating the relationship between career fit and project goals to resistant employees
e. By demonstrating the return on investment of the project
f. By individually approaching all resistant employees and attempting to convince them of the benefits of the project
g. All of the above

Employees, Technology, and Resistance to Change

As a project team member implementing an internal information technology (IT) project, one must somehow confront resistance to change. The solutions to resistance to change lie not within the IT project being implementing, but among the employees for which the project is being implemented. When working with employees, all of the above efforts and techniques mentioned in the chapter question can be used to confront resistance to change, although no one individual effort may be a solution in itself. Since there is no one-size-fits-all approach, taking only one specific action may not help, and may even create more resistance, unless the root cause of resistance to change is identified. As a project team member, when one encounters resistance to change, one should first start by surfacing the resistance explicitly and making sure that no resistance is ignored. Asking for constructive reasons why the change won't work, acting on feedback, or creating opportunities to acknowledge resistance are some of the ways of dealing with the resistance.

After having acknowledged the resistance, resistance should be named and categorized with the help of information gathered during a root cause analysis. The most common categorization used is as follows:

- Not knowing: Employees are not aware that a change is required, or how they are supposed to change.
- Not able: Employees are not capable of making the change (i.e., they need new skills).
- Not willing: Although those employees are aware that a change is required and though they may have the necessary skill sets, they are still resistant to change for other reasons.

Not Knowing:

Employees falling into this category are not aware that a change is required. A sense of urgency should be created in order to communicate that the status quo is no longer acceptable, as well as to establish a clear vision of where the company is going. Once those employees understand the shared vision and the need to change, moving forward is then much easier.

Visioning and informative workshops, as well as monthly or weekly newsletters, are effective responses for those "Not Knowing." During these workshops and in these newsletters, progress towards the company vision, and, if possible, return on investment of the project achieved so far, should be clearly stated. With the help of such efforts, employees in this category may give up resistance or move to the "Not Able" or "Not Willing" categories.

Not Able:

This type of resistance is more difficult to overcome than "Not Knowing". The "Not Able" employees need additional support to embrace change and the new project. Although "Not Able" employees are aware that change is required, they do not have the necessary skill sets to implement or work with the results of the change.

In order to assist those "Not Able", training and work-shadowing sessions may be held. With the help of work-shadowing sessions, employees not only learn the new business processes and the new software they are going to use, but they also get to build relationships with their users. Role models, the critical success factors in work-shadowing sessions, must be assigned to lead the implementation of the project. At the end of the change management efforts, those "Not Able" may give up resistance and embrace the change, or move to the "Not Willing" category.

Not Willing:

The "Not Willing" category of the resistance categories is the most challenging. Although those "Not Willing" are aware of the need for change and are capable of implementing it, they are still resistant to change for various reasons:

Reason 1: Those "not willing" do not agree with change

Imposing change without getting "Not Willing" employees' buy-in may further fuel their resistance to the change. To overcome disagreement, they should be actively involved in the IT project even before the kick-off meeting, and may even be assigned decision-making opportunities.

Reason 2: The change does not fit with the career goals of those "not willing"

Assume that an assistant manager is awaiting a promotion. Recently, she hears that with the implementation of a new IT project, three managerial positions will be merged into one. Upon hearing this, the assistant manager may likely be upset. To overcome demotivation and resistance, her career fit with the change should be explicitly stated. The assistant manager should be convinced that her role is not diminished and that there will be room for career development.

In the case of no opportunity for career development, or employee redundancy brought about by the implementation of the new IT project, an open strategy should be immediately adopted and discussed with the employees concerned. To ensure success of the IT project, key employees should be kept within the organization until the project is complete. In order to accomplish this, retention bonuses may be introduced. These bonuses, in addition to redundancy payments, encourage employees to stay within the organization and to contribute to the IT project until they are no longer required.

Reason 3: Those "not willing" are emotionally attached to old work habits

Those who are "Not Willing" may be attached to old work habits, or may become overly emotional when confronted with change. Consequently, they should be given the opportunity to adapt to the change slowly.

Reason 4: Those "not willing" are waiting for others to change first

Those who are "Not Willing" may be too cautious to take action. These employees need role models to provide motivation and to mirror appropriate behaviors. Quick-wins and role models will help ease their concerns.

Reason 5: Those "not willing" do not believe that change will actually happen

This kind of employee may be right that the company is implementing the wrong IT project at the wrong time. For instance, in an overly-saturated, competitive industry, implementing an IT project with the aim of customer acquisition will not succeed, causing the company to lose valuable time. In this case, "Not Willing" employees advocating customer retention IT projects should have been consulted. Although employees falling into this category may seem confrontational, their concerns may be valid ones. These employees' concerns must be taken into account and they must be given the opportunity to challenge the return on investment of the IT project.

Reason 6: Those "not willing" show resistance to change for the sake of their own interests

Employees falling into this category do not have goodwill towards the IT project and uphold their own priorities over the company's goals. Although this situation occurs very rarely, it may sometimes be necessary to terminate this kind of employee's participation in the project.

The sub-categories of those "not willing" can be easily extended, but no matter the case, it is important to take a one-on-one approach when addressing their issues and concerns. Explicit conversations should be held with those employees to determine their future fit with the change.

Resistance to Change Among Departments

In addition to resistance to change among employees, companies also often experience resistance to change among departments such as between business units and IT departments within the company. The solution to this type of resistance may be to develop operational level agreements (OLA) and performance measures between conflicting parties. According to the Information Technology Infrastructure Library (ITIL®), the definition of OLA is as follows:

"An operational level agreement (OLA) is a contract that defines how various IT groups within a company plan to deliver a service or a set of services." [ITIL®]

More important than setting targets, the aim of developing OLAs should be to establish a healthy platform for discussions and to create opportunities to come together in order to reach a common understanding and agreement on the future relationship between the two parties. Such an approach will result in OLAs being perceived as facilitative, customer-oriented agreements rather than prescriptive, contractual, enforceable arrangements. In addition, while developing an OLA, a "think-big-start-small" approach should be adopted, with the first priority given to quick-wins.

Even in the case of successful change management or OLA development initiatives, there are those who will always remain skeptical of the change. Such skeptics may have developed a selective memory about how effective old software or services used to be. The only way to convince this type of employee is to demonstrate the performance and cost improvements achieved by the implementation of the new software or service. In order to achieve this, performance and cost metrics of the old software or service must be gathered in advance, which is not easy.

One should never forget that change management is a people business, not a technical one. The completion of an IT project marks the beginning of a change management journey rather than its end. Although the techniques and efforts described in this chapter seem more related to project managers, all project team members should be aware of them and be prepared for the challenges ahead.

Software Testing Chapters

Chapter 6

The Relationship Between Software Testing and Road Traffic

Question

Place the items below in order of their importance, based on their effectiveness in establishing a healthy, efficient, and successful software testing practice in a company.

(Highest Priority 1 2 3 4 5 Lowest Priority)

- ___ Testing Tools
- ___ Testing Processes
- ___ Test Design Techniques
- ___ Testing Terminology and Culture of Quality
- ___ Testing Organization and Skills

The Relationship Between Software Testing and Road Traffic

This chapter will begin with an analogy between software testing and traffic in order to illustrate the order of importance of the items introduced in the chapter question.

Testing Terminology and Culture of Quality

The first and most important prerequisite for maintaining well-functioning road traffic is the presence of a common traffic terminology and culture of traffic safety. Without agreed-upon traffic signs and traffic rules, even well-established roads and brand new cars will not help traffic flow smoothly. For example, assume that every driver's perception of a "No U-Turn" sign is different, there is no uniform direction of traffic, and that traffic lights have no standard colors. The only and obvious outcome of this kind of road traffic is chaos. Even maintaining well-established traffic rules and standards is insufficient for ensuring well-functioning traffic, unless, of course, pedestrians and drivers heed these rules and standards.

The same is true of software testing. During an IT project, what if project team members had no common understanding of the software testing terminology used? The end result would surely be a chaotic, ineffective, and inefficient software testing practice, leading to buggy software. Even with a well-defined, company-wide software testing terminology, gaining buy-in regarding the implementation of this terminology from every project team member is still needed to ensure that software testing terms are employed accurately.

Based on the assertion that gaining buy-in for standard software testing terminology from every project team member is important, any software testing initiative should first be handled as a people issue rather than a technology issue. All project team members should be involved in the software testing initiative in order to encourage them to embrace quality. Otherwise, project team members may raise questions such as: "Do we really need software testing?", "Isn't software testing a cost center?" or "Since we have a test team in place, why don't we submit the code without conducting any unit testing?" Such questions may lead to the failure of the software testing initiative. In order to prevent this kind of failure, project team members should change their mindsets to create a culture of quality whose motto is "Quality is not tested, but built." Every project team member should be encouraged to embrace this culture of quality and integrate testing and quality into every activity of the IT project, beginning with the project kick-off meeting and continuing through the business analysis, system analysis, development, deployment, and support activities.

Testing Processes

After having established common software testing terminology and a culture of quality among project team members, testing processes must next be implemented. Further analysis of the analogy between software testing and road traffic can illustrate how testing processes might be regarded as highways. In road traffic, where well-established roads are absent, the existence of new and powerful high-speed cars does not prevent traffic accidents. This kind of traffic is completely dependent on the competence of the drivers and pedestrians. Any one mistake made by a driver or pedestrian may potentially create a domino effect, causing a traffic jam, and therefore complete chaos.

This is also true of software testing. Without well-defined software testing processes, the success of software testing depends on the competence of individuals involved in the testing. In this environment, tests are often developed in an ad hoc way, and under pressure, testers are usually ignored or over committed. Since there is no company-wide know-how shared among project team members and testers, successes are difficult to repeat, and lessons learned are infrequent. These unsuccessful practices do not leave room for systematic practices, continuous improvements, and test processes such as test monitoring, planning and control, test analysis, test design, test implementation, test execution, the evaluation of test exit criteria and reporting, and test closure activities. Since the practice depends mostly on individuals, it is not healthy and sustainable.

54

Testing Organization and Skills

Assuming that highways are built, and that drivers and pedestrians are properly trained in traffic rules and signs and understand the importance of maintaining a healthy traffic flow, drivers would then need to be given licenses. A licensed driver has passed a driving test and has the necessary skills and knowledge to operate a motorized vehicle. The type of driver's license establishes the roles and responsibilities of the driver. For example, in the United States, a "Class B Commercial Driver's License" (CDL) is a requirement for heavy and tractor-trailer truck drivers and bus drivers. A driver possessing a Class B CDL must have skills required for gear shifting and vehicle control, backing up, parking and docking, loading and unloading, and highway driving of commercial trucks that have an attached cab and cargo area with a combined weight greater than 26,000 pounds. Therefore, the requirements of obtaining a specific class of driver's license clearly set the expectations of the driver, as well as her roles and responsibilities.

Similar to different classes of driver's licenses, specific job titles used in testing organization, such as test analyst, technical test analyst, and usability tester, clearly establish the software tester roles and responsibilities. For example, a software tester whose title is "test analyst" is expected to be able to carry out black-box tests. Test analysts should be able to understand the requirement documents, derive test cases from use cases, generate test data from actual customer data, and apply black-box testing techniques and requirements coverage metrics. Likewise, a software tester whose title is "technical test analyst" is expected to be able to carry out white-box tests. Technical test analysts should be able to understand the inner workings of the software, understand system design documents, read pseudocode, generate test cases from code flow, and apply white-box testing techniques and code coverage metrics. The list can be easily extended to other titles such as test manager, automation tester, and usability tester.

As illustrated above, by clearly defining job titles, expectations of a software tester are established, and the boundaries of the software testing profession are drawn. Without outlining the expectations of software testers, neither their performance nor their skill set improvement areas can be measured. For example, a test manager may ask her technical test analysts to learn Swift programming language in order to conduct white-box tests in iOS environments, but she cannot request the same skill set from the test analysts on her team. Similarly, without drawing boundaries for software testers, they may be perceived as an all-in-one employee expected to deliver multiple types of tasks which may be irrelevant or inappropriate for their skill set. For example, returning to the road traffic analogy, asking a test analyst to develop tests to achieve 100% decision coverage is as inappropriate as asking a driver possessing a motorcycle driver's license to drive a bus.

Test Design Techniques

Imagine that there is now a well-established traffic infrastructure with 10-lane highways, trained pedestrians, licensed drivers, and sensory traffic lights. What if a snowstorm hits the city? In a snowstorm, a driver must forget everything she knows about driving a car on a sunny day. For example, the reflex of pushing the brake pedal in order to stop or slow down the car now might be a mistake, causing the car to skid into another car. Instead of pressing the brake pedal while driving on a snow-covered road, one should instead use engine braking to stop the car and prevent any quick maneuvers. Engine braking on a snow-covered road is easier said than done and is a good example of an advanced driving technique about which a driver should be knowledgeable.

As in the case of a snowstorm, software testing and software testing teams are under pressure and exposed to many constraints such as time, budget, and personnel constraints. In these stressful and error-prone work environments, software testers should be aware of different test design techniques and when to apply them. Employing appropriate test design techniques at the appropriate time will help software testers conduct their tests more efficiently and effectively. For example, test analysts should be able to apply black-box test design techniques such as equivalence partitioning, boundary value analysis, decision tables, and state transitions; technical test analysts should be able to apply white-box test design techniques such as statement coverage, decision coverage, and condition coverage. Using test design techniques will help software testers optimize their efforts.

Testing Tools

To continue the analogy between software testing and road traffic, imagine that the driver now has everything she needs, from a driver's license to knowledge of advanced driving techniques. The only missing item is a car. It is time to buy a car. Had the driver purchased a car in the absence of well-designed roads and without knowing how to drive, the inevitable result would be a fatal accident.

The same is true for software testing projects. Testing tools will only be useful when the organization has good testing processes, a common understanding of testing terminology and trained testers. Without these factors, the company's testing efforts are likely to become ineffective and inefficient, leading to an unsuccessful software testing practice due to an inefficient usage of tools.

To sum up, in order to establish and maintain a healthy and well-functioning software testing practice which utilizes resources effectively and efficiently, a company must implement the items below in the prescribed order:

1. Testing Terminology and Culture of Quality
2. Testing Processes
3. Testing Organization and Skills
4. Test Design Techniques
5. Testing Tools

Chapter 7

Risk and Software Testing: How Much Testing Is Enough?

Question
Which one of the following risks should be prioritized first in software testing? Note that the score 1 indicates the highest, and 5 indicates the lowest.

	Impact	Probability
Risk A	3	3
Risk B	1	4
Risk C	2	3
Risk D	5	2
Risk E	2	4

Risk and Software Testing: How Much Testing Is Enough?

How does one decide how much software testing is enough? Clearly, the amount of software testing conducted depends on the amount of risk involved. In this context, risk is defined as:

"The effect of uncertainty on objectives." [ISO 31000]

There are many types of risks, but the most prominent ones related to software testing are project and product risks. According to the 5th edition of the *PMBOK® Guide*, the definition of project risk is as follows:

"An uncertain event or condition that, if it occurs, has a positive or negative effect on one or more project objectives such as scope, schedule, cost, or quality." [PMBOK® Guide 5ᵗʰ Edition]

According to the ISTQB® Glossary, the definition of product risk is as follows:

"A risk directly related to the test object."
[ISTQB® Glossary]

From these definitions, which one of the above risks, project and product, is the responsibility of the test team? When considering project risks, it is obviously not possible for test teams to test the budget or deadlines of a project. Project risks can only be managed, not tested. Still, mitigating actions can be taken to minimize the effects of project risks. Only product risks can be tested. A software tester may wonder how product risks are tested. What are the points of reference for product risk? How are the expected results of product risks defined? The answer lies within the requirement specifications. Functional and non-functional requirements are the points of reference for different types of product risks as shown in the following list:

- Functionality
- Usability
- Performance
- Security
- Reliability
- Interoperability

- Compatibility
- Maintainability

The amount of software testing conducted depends on the amount of risk involved with the item to be tested. The formula for calculating the value of a risk is as follows:

Risk = Impact x Probability

In the above formula, impact of a risk means the estimated effect on the system and the business if the risk is realized, and probability of a risk means its likelihood of occurrence. Since impact and probability are completely different categories, their values must be multiplied in order to calculate the overall value of a risk. Based on this formula, the risk value of each risk mentioned in the chapter question is as follows:

- Risk A = 3 x 3 = 9
- Risk B = 1 x 4 = 4
- Risk C = 2 x 3 = 6
- Risk D = 5 x 2 = 10
- Risk E = 2 x 4 = 8

According to the definition in the chapter question, a smaller numerical value indicates more risk. Risk B, with a value of four, is the riskiest item on this list. This means that features related to Risk B should be tested more extensively by using stronger test design techniques. During software testing projects, in order to identify which test design technique should be applied to which feature, risks should be distributed on a quadrant according to their impact and likelihood scores, with the x-axis representing "impact" and the y-axis representing "probability," as shown in the following:

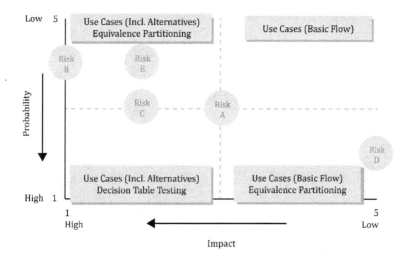

Figure 7.1 Risk quadrant diagram

In the above quadrant, weak test design techniques such as use case testing (basic flow) are applied to low-impact risks, while strong techniques, such as decision table testing, are applied to high-impact, high-probability risks.

As seen from the above risk calculations, risk assessment only requires simple arithmetic–specifically, the multiplication of impact and probability values. On the other hand, identifying risks and their impact and probability values is much more challenging and requires consensus among project team members. The techniques below can be used to identify risks and their values:
- Expert interviews
- Past experiences (Lessons learned)
- Checklists
- Brainstorming
- Risk workshops

The more project team members that are involved in the process of risk identification, the better the result will be. At the end of risk identification sessions, risk categories, risks under each category, and their impact and probability scores can be identified. A sample risk identification table for online banking can be seen as follows:

Risk Category: Functionality		Impact (1 highest, 5 lowest)	Probability (1 highest, 5 lowest)
Functionality Risk 1	Users cannot submit complaint form	4	4
Functionality Risk 2	Users cannot calculate the interest accurately	1	5
Risk Category: Performance		**Impact (1 highest, 5 lowest)**	**Probability (1 highest, 5 lowest)**
Performance Risk 1	Response time is longer than 2 seconds at 100 concurrent users	2	2
Performance Risk 2	System fails at 300 concurrent users	2	3
Risk Category: Usability		**Impact (1 highest, 5 lowest)**	**Probability (1 highest, 5 lowest)**
Usability Risk 1	The order of 'OK' and 'Cancel' buttons is not consistent among user interfaces	3	2

Table 7.1 A sample risk identification table for online banking

It is easily seen from the table above that the most important risk is Performance Risk 1, as that has a score of 4.

A More Thorough Risk Assessment
To conduct a more thorough risk assessment, the impact of a risk can be divided into two different categories:
- Severity: system impact
- Priority: business impact

A software tester may wonder why there is a need to handle the impact in more detail. Aren't severity and priority correlated? Generally, severity and priority are correlated, but there are exceptional cases in which they are not. For example, assume that a customer has received a credit card statement from her bank. The customer then verifies all expenditures. However, the logo on the credit card statement belongs to another bank. The customer now doubts that it is her credit card's statement. The customer then checks every item, including her name, credit card number, and address on the statement. Although all details again appear to be accurate, the customer then phones the call center. It takes ten minutes to clarify the issue, which appears to be a minor bug in the credit card system. Instead of printing "Logo_1.jpg" on the credit card statement, "Logo_2.jpg" was printed.

In order to more accurately assess such a case, it is appropriate to use two different impact ratings: severity and priority. In the case of the credit card statement, the values for each would probably appear as follows:
- Severity (system impact): 5   (1 highest, 5 lowest)
- Priority (business impact): 2   (1 highest, 5 lowest)

From the system's point of view, since the error is a minor bug in the system and can be easily fixed, it should be assigned the score 5. From the customer's point of view, however, this bug creates confusion. Although it is not as important as a miscalculated amount, the error nevertheless irritates the customer, causing her to query the issue by contacting the call center, and thereby incurring additional cost to the company. Consequently, the error should be assigned a score of at least 2.

Although handling the impact of risk by using two different categories makes the risk identification process more complex, it provides a more accurate assessment. By using these new impact categories, a new risk value can be calculated as follows:

$$Risk = Severity \times Priority \times Probability$$

In general, while calculating the impact of a risk, the items below should be taken into consideration:
- Usage intensity
- Damage to be caused
- Cost of rework
- Legal sanctions

Probability indicates a calculation of a risk's likelihood of occurrence. The items below should be taken into consideration when calculating probability:

- Defect history
- Complexity
- New development
- Interrelationship
- Size
- Technology
- Geographical spread
- Inexperience of the team
- Frequency of usage

In risk-based testing, risk identification and risk assessment should be followed by risk mitigation measures. Mitigation measures are not limited to software testing; they may also include redesigning the software and maintaining the operation of outdated systems.

To sum up, product risks allow the test team to determine the appropriate test design techniques and test effort estimations, as well as to guide the test team throughout the project. When evaluating risks, the steps below should be taken:

a. Risk identification
b. Risk assessment
c. Risk mitigation

Chapter 8

The Relationship Between Software Test Design Techniques and High Jump Techniques

Which women's high jump Olympic record was broken by using the "Scissors" technique at the 1928 summer Olympics?

   a. 1.10 m
   b. 1.27 m
   c. 1.59 m
   d. 1.98 m
   e. 2.06 m
   f. 2.37 m

Scissors Technique
Ethel Catherwood at 1928 Summer Olympics

Which women's high jump Olympic record was broken by using the "Fosbury Flop" technique at the 2004 summer Olympics?

   a. 1.10 m
   b. 1.27 m
   c. 1.59 m
   d. 1.98 m
   e. 2.06 m
   f. 2.37 m

Fosbury Flop technique

The Relationship Between Software Test Design Techniques and High Jump Techniques

Answers to the chapter question concerning the high jump Olympic record results may be found below:

The women's high jump Olympic record broken at the 1928 Summer Olympics was 1.59 m, and 2.06 m at the 2004 Summer Olympics.

Why might there be such a big difference —almost a half-meter— between each Olympic record? Is it because of:

- Technological developments in athletic footwear?
- Improvements in track surfaces?
- Developments in training and workout practices?
- Enhanced nutritional guidelines for athletes?
- An increase in athletes' height?
- All of the above
- None of the above

One may assume that all of the above factors would result in a positive impact on the improvement of the high jump Olympic record. But although all factors may have an effect, none of these factors alone can explain the drastic improvement of 47 cm. The reason behind the significant improvement, then, must lie in the change from the "Scissors" to the "Fosbury Flop" high jump techniques.

If the above is true, then why did athletes not always use the "Fosbury Flop" technique? In science and sports, when faced with a problem, people generally tend to copy behaviors, forms, and techniques from nature. Most probably, while athletes were tackling the question of how to jump over a bar, they looked to horses. Athletes may have observed the jumping pattern of horses during hurdle races and then simply copied this pattern in their own high jump practices. But athletes may have overlooked one important fact: since horses have four legs, they must pass their front legs over the obstacle first. This is not true for human beings; having two legs, human beings are free to hurdle over an obstacle with their entire body, rather than legs-first. The first athlete who recognized this flexibility was Dick Fosbury; by changing his technique, Dick Fosbury broke many men's high jump records and ignited a revolution, then an evolution, in the high jump discipline. Today, all high jump athletes use this technique, which has become the *de jure* high jump technique in the Olympic games.

Using the right techniques in software testing is as important as in athletics. Due to budget and time constraints, sufficient effort is usually not allocated to software testing, and these constraints can often be used as excuses for missing bugs in the software. However, alternatives for better, more efficient tests should be investigated before hastily placing blame on any one party. One solution may be using appropriate software test design techniques. Below, a simple calculator case study will be analyzed in order to show how success can be achieved in software testing efforts by using the appropriate test design techniques.

Assume that a very simple calculator which only accepts one-digit negative or positive integers and can perform only four simple operations, is being tested. The algorithm of the calculator works as follows:

(input X) (four operations) (input Y) = (output Z)

Z is the result of any four operations on two integers, X and Y.

The calculator may be tested by posing the following question:

Question:
How many test cases are required to test every input combination of this calculator?

Answer:
To find the answer, all that is needed is basic math knowledge and good reasoning:

(input X) (four operations) (input Y) = (output Z)

- **Input X:** Due to the input constraint, X accepts only one-digit negative or positive integers. So integers -9, -8, -7, -6, -5, -4, -3, -2, -1, 0, 1, 2, 3, 4, 5, 6, 7, 8, 9 can be entered as inputs—a total of **19 different inputs.**

- **Four operations:** Addition, subtraction, multiplication, division—a total of **4 different inputs**.
- **Input Y:** Due to the input constraint, Y accepts only one-digit negative or positive integers. So integers -9, -8, -7, -6, -5, -4, -3, -2, -1, 0, 1, 2, 3, 4, 5, 6, 7, 8, 9 can be entered as inputs—a total of **19 different inputs**.

Since all of the input combinations are included in the question, the number of test cases required can now be easily calculated by taking the Cartesian product of three sets: input X, four operations, and input Y:

Number of test cases = 19 x 4 x 19 = 1444

Are there too many required test cases in this example? Are all 1444 test cases necessary in order to perform a successful test of the calculator?

How effective would running the following four test cases be?

- **Test Case A**
  Test step 1: X= 3,
  Test step 2: operation= "addition",
  Test step 3: Y= 5

  Expected result: 8

- **Test Case B**
  Test step 1: X= 7,
  Test step 2: operation= "addition",
  Test step 3: Y= 2

  Expected result: 9

- **Test Case C**
  Test step 1: X= 8,
  Test step 2: operation= "addition",
  Test step 3: Y= 1

  Expected result: 9

- **Test Case D**
  Test step 1: X= 6,
  Test step 2: operation= "addition",
  Test step 3: Y= 6

  Expected result: 12

After examining the above examples, it is clear that running all four test cases is unnecessary. Since the above four test cases are all testing the same combination type, a combination of positive integers in the "addition" operation, running any more after the first one would only add minor value to the testing effort. Assume, during a test project, that a software tester had limited time and would be able to run a total of only 10 test cases. In this case, it would not be wise for the software tester to spend all of her time running the same kind of test cases. Instead, the software tester should diversify her test cases by trying other combinations as well. By doing so, the software tester will gain a broader understanding of the quality of the software and find more bugs.

If the software tester does not diversify her test cases, the software tester's efforts are like killing mosquitos in only one part of the marshland while allowing others to live. To rid a marshland from mosquitos, a software tester would have to partition the marshland and apply at least one pesticide to each one of the partitions, as shown in the figure below:

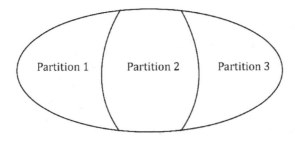

Figure 8.1 Sample partitions

Parallel to the marshland analogy, software also has partitions, and mosquitos as well. In the calculator case study, the mosquitos are obvious; they are the bugs in the code which lead to miscalculations. Partitions are trickier to identify. A partition might be defined as:

"A portion of an input or output domain for which the behavior of a component or system is assumed to be the same, based on the specification."
[ISTQB® Glossary]

What, then, are the partitions in the calculator case study? The partitions in the calculator case study may be represented as follows, beginning with input X:

(input X) (four operations) (input Y) = (output Z)

- **Partitions of input X**
  a. Positive integers
  b. Zero
  c. Negative integers

  A total of **3 partitions**

- **Partitions of four operations**
  a. Addition
  b. Subtraction
  c. Multiplication
  d. Division

  A total of **4 partitions**

- **Partitions of input Y**
  a. Positive integers
  b. Zero
  c. Negative integers

  A total of **3 partitions**

In order to identify the number of test cases which would cover each possible combination of partitions at least once, the Cartesian product of three partition sets should be taken:

Number of test cases = 3 x 4 x 3 = 36

Reducing the number of test cases from 1444 to 36 results in a huge gain in terms of time and effort. By dividing the software inputs into partitions, the testing approach becomes more structured and robust. The test design technique used in this case is called the "Equivalence Partitioning" technique and its type is called "Strong Normal", and the objective is to increase the coverage of partition combinations by running a minimum number of test cases. In this case, when a software tester runs 36 different test cases by selecting one representative value set from each different partition combination, she covers each partition combination at least once, achieving 100% partition combination coverage.

In some cases, even when a software tester achieves 100% coverage of one aspect, she may still not feel confident in the results and may question whether 100% coverage of this is sufficient. Having achieved a specific coverage percentage should not prevent a software tester from running additional test cases. If a software tester believes that she needs more test cases for specific test inputs or to spot flaws in the software, she should run additional test cases, depending on the situation. The aim of establishing a coverage percentage with the help of test design techniques is to understand the thoroughness of the testing of one aspect, but there are always other aspects to explore. The rest depends on the software tester.

Chapter 9

Black-box Testing Versus White-box Testing

Question
Which one of the statements below describes the difference between black-box testing and white-box testing?

a. While black-box test cases are negative tests, white-box test cases are positive tests

b. While black-box test cases test non-functional attributes of the software, white-box test cases test functional attributes

c. While programming knowledge is required for running black-box test cases, it is NOT required for running white-box test cases

d. While black-box test cases are keyword-driven, white-box test cases are data-driven

e. While black-box test cases consider the external behavior of the software and examine what the system is supposed to do, white-box test cases consider the internal behavior of the software and examine how the system does what it is supposed to do

f. All of the above

g. None of the above

Black-box Testing Versus White-box Testing

The correct answer to this chapter's question is option e. As its name indicates, black-box testing perceives software as a closed box and does not consider its inner workings. This kind of testing evaluates software from the user's point of view using the requirement specifications as its test basis. By using requirement specifications, input combinations are generated, and outputs are compared with the expected results. While generating test cases, both functional and non-functional requirements can be used as the test basis. A basic black-box test case example may be seen below:

Functional Requirement 1
User selects credit card type *(Related business rule: Number '1' stands for Visa, number '2' stands for MasterCard, and number '3' stands for American Express)*

Based on the above functional requirement, the following black-box test case can be generated:

Test Case Name	Test Case of Requirement 1
Step 1	Go to credit card payment page
Step 2	Select number 2 from drop-down list
Step 3	Press submit button
Expected Result	Credit card type field is displayed as 'MasterCard'

In black-box testing, test cases are usually generated from requirement specifications and the input/output combinations are used to determine the appropriate test data. The software tester is unaware of the inner workings or the algorithm of the system being tested. A software tester may wonder why white-box test cases are necessary in this case. Before settling on an answer, the following pseudocode of the system being tested should be examined:

```
READ NUMBER
IF NUMBER == 1 THEN
          PRINT "Visa"
END IF
IF NUMBER == 2 THEN
          PRINT "MasterCard"
END IF
IF NUMBER == 3 THEN
          PRINT "American Express"
END IF
IF NUMBER == 4 THEN
          PRINT "Visa"
END IF
```

The above pseudocode is a surprising one. Although a fourth option does not exist in the "Functional Requirement 1", the software developer has voluntarily inserted this option into the pseudocode. It is the duty of the software tester, in this case, to argue that the insertion of this extra code is unnecessary because it is not mentioned in the requirement specifications. The software tester knows that developing a feature not mentioned in the requirements only creates complications and confusion. By the time this extra option is realized, however, it may be too late. In the above test case example, the black-box software tester will not include the fourth simply because she may not anticipate such a violation made by the software developer. Nevertheless, such violations occur because, due to the different points of view among different project team members (especially between business analysts and software developers), requirements may deviate from their initial definitions. The following Venn diagram show how code deviates from requirements in time:

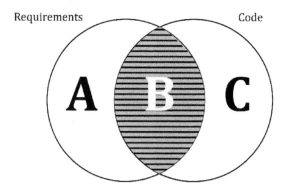

Requirements   Code

Figure 9.1 Deviation of code from requirements

From this diagram, it may be easily inferred that although A and B are expected to be coded, B and C are coded instead. This signifies a major shift from what should be coded to what actually *is* coded, which in turn, signifies a major shift in requirements implementation. Thus, relying only on black-box test cases, which focus solely on requirement specifications, will result in unsuccessful or incomplete software testing. In order to achieve successful software testing, white-box test cases (which focus on code and the internal behavior of the software) should also be generated and executed. By doing so, the coverage metrics can be extended from requirements coverage to code coverage.

The Basic Code Coverage Criteria: Statement Coverage and Decision Coverage

The basic code coverage criteria of white-box testing are "statement coverage" and "decision coverage." As defined by the ISTQB® Certified Tester Foundation Level Syllabus Version 2011, "statement coverage" is "the number of executable statements covered by test cases divided by the number of all executable statements in the code under test" while "decision coverage" is "the number of decision outcomes covered by test cases divided by the number of all possible decision outcomes in the code under test."

It is a widely-known fact that decision coverage is stronger than statement coverage; 100% decision coverage guarantees 100% statement coverage, but not vice versa. To verify this fact, and to better understand white-box testing, the question below will be examined:

Question:
Considering the following pseudocode, calculate the minimum number of test cases for 100% statement coverage, and the minimum number of test cases for 100% decision coverage, respectively.

```
READ A
READ B
READ C
IF C > A THEN
        IF C > B THEN
                PRINT "C must be bigger than A and B"
        ENDIF
ELSE
        PRINT "B can be smaller than C"
ENDIF
```

    a.   Statement Coverage = 2, Decision Coverage = 4.
    b.   Statement Coverage = 3, Decision Coverage = 3.
    c.   Statement Coverage = 2, Decision Coverage = 3.
    d.   Statement Coverage = 3, Decision Coverage = 2.

Solution:
In order to solve this question, it is better to draw a flowchart diagram of the pseudocode. When drawing the diagram, common flowchart symbols can be adopted, where a rectangle represents a statement (process), and a diamond represents a decision (if).

Statement Coverage
To find the statement coverage, the question below should be posed:

Reading the flowchart diagram from top to bottom, how many test cases would be needed to ensure that each rectangle (statement) is reached at least once?

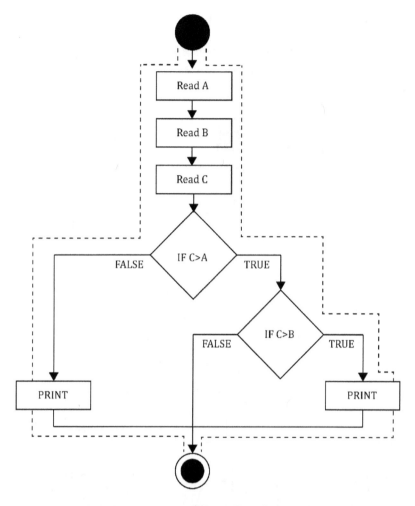

Figure 9.2 Flow chart diagram of the pseudocode
(Dotted lines representing statement coverage)

As shown by the two dotted lines in the flowchart, two test cases will cover all of the statements. For example:

Test Case 1: A=3; B=4; C=5;
Test Case 2: A=5; B=2; C=3;

Decision Coverage

To find the decision coverage, the question below should be posed:

Reading the flowchart diagram from top to bottom, how many test cases would be needed to ensure that every outcome of each diamond (decision) is reached at least once?

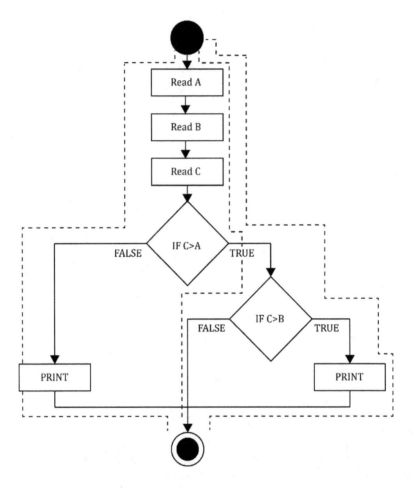

Figure 9.3 Flow chart diagram of the pseudocode
(Dotted lines representing decision coverage)

As shown by the three dotted lines in the flowchart, three test cases will cover all the decision outcomes (True and False). For example:

Test Case 1: A=3; B=4; C=5;

Test Case 2: A=5; B=2; C=3;
Test Case 2: A=3; B=6; C=5;

The correct answer to the coverage question is that a minimum of two test cases must be executed in order to achieve 100% statement coverage, and a minimum of three test cases must be executed in order to achieve 100% decision coverage, which is the option c in the question. Since the test cases needed for 100% decision coverage include the test cases needed for 100% statement coverage, the claim that decision coverage is stronger than statement coverage is correct. This also means that 100% decision coverage guarantees 100% statement coverage, but not vice versa.

In the case of white-box testing, the solution to the question clearly illustrates the purpose of white-box testing (testing the internal behavior of the software) which is the option e in the chapter question.

The need for both black-box and white-box testing in the software industry also affects career paths in software testing. According to the ISTQB® roadmap for software testers, while software testers responsible for conducting black-box tests are called "test analysts," software testers responsible for conducting white-box tests are called "technical test analysts." A software tester may wonder which testing method is more successful. The answer is neither. As stated in option e in the chapter question, while black-box test cases consider the external behavior of the software and examine what the system is supposed to do, white-box test cases consider the internal behavior of the software and examine how the system does what it is supposed to do. Therefore, both black-box testing and white-box testing can be said to complement each other.

Chapter 10

To Automate or Not to Automate: How Much Test Automation Is Enough?

Question
What percentage of test cases should be automated?
   a. In order to increase testing efficiency and effectiveness, 100% of test cases should be automated
   b. More than 50% of test cases should be automated
   c. Test cases should be automated as much as possible, within budget, time, and resource constraints
   d. Manual testing is more successful than test automation; therefore, there is no need for test automation
   e. None of the above

To Automate or Not to Automate: How Much Test Automation Is Enough?

Currently, test automation is becoming more popular among test teams. However, many issues surrounding test automation remain unclear. For example:

- How does one automate test cases?
- Which tool would best satisfy test automation needs?
- Is it possible to automate all test cases?
- What should the proper test automation approach be? Data-driven, or keyword-driven test automation?

It is obvious that the above questions mostly focus on *how* to automate instead of *what* to automate. It is difficult to decide *how* to automate without first knowing or identifying *what* to automate. But most test teams overlook this fact. Test teams may even try to automate *all* of their test cases and therefore, in the end, fail in their test automation endeavors. This problem raises the following important question: Is it logical to automate all test cases? Is it even feasible? Which test cases should be automated? To elaborate on these questions, the issue will be analyzed by using the following criteria:

- Test execution frequency
- Maturity of the system under test (SUT)

In the following quadrant, "test execution frequency" is represented by the x-axis, with "maturity of the SUT" represented by the y-axis.

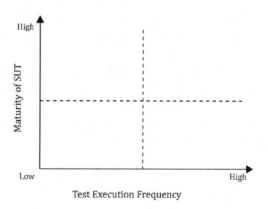

Figure 10.1 Test execution frequency and maturity of SUT

Test Execution Frequency

Test execution frequency is one of the most important factors affecting how much test automation is to be carried out. The higher test execution frequency the SUT has, the more justification for the tests to be automated because of the savings in manual test execution time.

Test execution frequency of the SUT is dependent on the regression testing needs of the SUT. As the need for regression testing increases, the test execution frequency increases. An SUT that is easily affected by changes in other features of the software often has a higher regression testing need than those other features. A traceability matrix can be used to calculate the impact of changes that will require regression testing.

Maturity of the SUT

Another important factor that affects how much test automation should be implemented is the SUT's maturity level. Test automation is a software development project. A software tester may argue that while using record/playback tools, no software development is needed. However, even if a software tester uses a record/playback testing tool, some sort of code is being generated behind the scenes. Whether or not a software tester manipulates this code, it is nevertheless there.

Since test automation is a software development project, requirements of the SUT (similar to software development which needs requirements) are also needed for test automation. An SUT that is not mature has unstable requirements that are being changed, updated and removed. When the test automation effort is attempted with an unstable SUT, the effort will probably fail, or will soon become redundant, resulting in wasted time and effort. The maturity level of the SUT is inversely proportional to the frequency of change requests implemented in the SUT.

The more mature the SUT is, the more justification for the tests to be automated.

Test Automation Prioritization

In order to prioritize the SUTs according to their suitability for automation, the quadrant drawn for the analysis of SUTs can be divided into four sections ("High", "Medium", "Medium" and "Low"), as shown below:

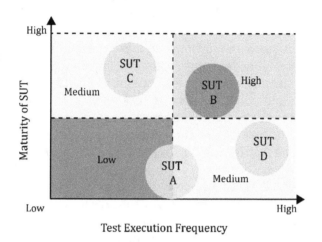

Figure 10.2 Test automation prioritization quadrant

High – High Priority SUTs for Test Automation
(High Maturity, High Frequency)

SUTs that fall into this category have high maturity levels and high test execution frequencies. This means that SUTs in this category are stable and are frequently tested. For example, consider the check balance feature of an online banking system. Since the check balance feature operates by a well-defined process, this feature and its requirements are not likely to be modified, thus resulting in a high maturity level.

As for its test execution frequency, due to its essential nature, the check balance feature is strongly connected to other features of the system, meaning that any change to any other feature of the software would trigger the need to retest it, thus resulting in a high test execution frequency.

With high maturity levels and high test execution frequencies, SUTs which have similar nature as the check balance feature are high priority candidates for test automation.

Medium – Medium Priority SUTs for Test Automation (Low Maturity, High Frequency)

Although SUTs falling into this category have high test execution frequencies, they have low maturity levels. For example, assume that a project team is working on the customer facing reporting feature of an online banking system. Unfortunately, the business units are still unsure about which content to display, how to display the content, and which charts to use in the reporting feature. Business units are constantly submitting change requests regarding the reporting feature. These change requests will result in revisions to the reporting feature, leading to a decrease in its maturity level.

From a technical point of view, in contrast, since the reporting feature of an online banking system retrieves data from almost all other features of the software and is easily affected by the changes in other features, any change to any other feature will trigger a need to retest the reporting feature, thus resulting in a high test execution frequency.

Although SUTs falling into this category will require revisions, the time and effort spent in making these changes may be worth the investment in test automation, since these kinds of SUTs are tested frequently. SUTs falling into this category hold a medium priority in test automation.

Medium – Medium Priority SUTs for Test Automation (High Maturity, Low Frequency)

Although SUTs falling into this category have high maturity levels, they have low test execution frequencies. For example, take an international wire transfer feature of an online banking system. This feature has a well-defined process flow and internationally agreed-upon data field definitions, thus resulting in a high maturity level.

From a technical point of view, due to its stand-alone nature, the international wire transfer feature is probably loosely connected to other features of the system, preventing it from being affected by the changes in other features, thus resulting in low test execution frequencies.

Although SUTs falling into this category have low test execution frequencies, their high maturity levels may be worth the investment in test automation. SUTs falling into this category hold medium priority in test automation.

Low – Low Priority SUTs for Test Automation (Low Maturity, Low Frequency)

Assume that a project team is working on adding a nice-to-have feature to the online banking user preference page (e.g., a feature allowing users to change their screen's background color). The business unit demanding this feature has submitted several change requests regarding the feature, and the project team expects them to continue to submit more. Never-ending change requests are negatively affecting the maturity level of this feature, thus resulting in low maturity levels.

Because of its stand-alone nature, the user preference feature has a low dependency on other features and has a low test execution frequency. As a result, the time and effort spent on automating these kinds of SUTs are not worth the investment. SUTs falling into this category will not be automated. Undertaking manual testing is sufficient for covering these test cases. SUTs falling into this category hold low priority in test automation.

When prioritizing test cases for test automation, the question of *what* to automate should logically be followed by *how* to automate (including a definition of the test automation requirements). Otherwise, testing tool vendors may drive the testing tool selection and implementation efforts. Testing tool vendors may try to convince the test team to purchase a tool by offering elaborate demos, sending invitations to conferences, and by offering free trial software licenses. None of these methods, however, makes sense unless the test team is sure about the company's test automation requirements. Before purchasing a testing tool, the test team should ensure that the following goals are met:

- Clearly define the company's test automation objectives and requirements.
- Match the company's test automation requirements with tool capabilities, and avoid unnecessary licensing costs.
- Know the technology constraints of the testing tool.
- Conduct market research for both commercial and open-source tools.
- Ask for RFIs (Request for Information) from commercial tool vendors.
- Based on the requirements and the RFI responses, create a short list of tool vendors.
- Ask for RFPs (Request for Proposal) from commercial tool vendors.
- Ask for POCs (Proof of Concept) from commercial tool vendors.
- Visit commercial tool vendors' clients in the field.
- Remember that testing tools are also software and can have bugs. Evaluate each testing tool's support fees, support processes, and training costs.

Even though the team has conducted its research and is ready for implementation of the testing tool, the test team should nevertheless take the following into consideration:
- Do not automate for the sake of automation.
- To prevent missing test cases and to increase test efficiency, pay attention to the test case naming/numbering conventions.
- Focus on the value of test cases instead of their quantity.
- Do not forget that test automation is a software development project; thus, seek buy-in and help from software developers.
- Choose software testers who possess technical backgrounds.
- Do not adopt only the record/playback approach for test automation. Employ verification points, and make use of data and keyword-driven frameworks.
- Develop maintainable test scripts.

Usability Chapters

Chapter 11

User Experience (UX) and Usability

Question

Which of the statements below best describes the relationship between user experience (UX) and usability?

    a.   User experience (UX) is a subset of usability

    b.   There are commonalities between usability and UX

    c.   Usability and UX are entirely different professions which do not have any commonalities

    d.   Usability is a subset of UX

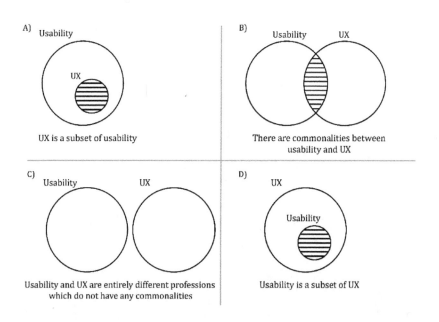

A) Usability — UX

UX is a subset of usability

B) Usability — UX

There are commonalities between usability and UX

C) Usability — UX

Usability and UX are entirely different professions which do not have any commonalities

D) UX — Usability

Usability is a subset of UX

User Experience (UX) and Usability

Each assertion made in the above chapter question shall be explored below:

Assertion A – UX is a subset of usability.

Usability

UX is a subset of usability

Those who support the above assertion may express the arguments below:

- Contrary to UX, which is comprised of only qualitative attributes, usability consists of both qualitative and quantitative attributes, which makes usability a superset of user experience.
- Usable products/services are easy to use and learn, and they have high-quality UX. Thus, UX is a part of usability.
- In order to produce a usable product or service, a company should first create a high-quality UX.
- Currently, most companies operating in the same industry provide the same functionalities and features; in order to differentiate themselves, companies should focus on the usability aspects of their products and services. Functionality, UX, performance, security and all other non-functional requirements are the pillars of usability.

Assertion B – There are commonalities between usability and UX.

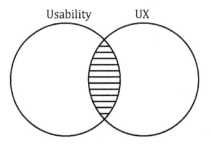

There are commonalities between
usability and UX

Those who support the above assertion may express the arguments below:

- Usability and UX have commonalities only in the emotional aspects of graphic design.
- While usability takes into consideration quantitative disciplines like interaction design, information architecture, and information design, UX focuses on qualitative disciplines such as cognitive memory and sub-consciousness, which affect human emotions and graphic design. Usability and UX are very different in nature and share only minor commonalities.
- The commonalities between UX and usability only exist in graphic design. In other disciplines, their differences become more apparent.

Assertion C – Usability and UX are entirely different professions which do not share any commonalities.

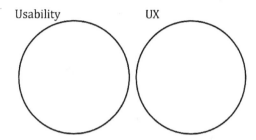

Usability and UX are entirely different professions
which do not have any commonalities

Those who support the above assertion may express the arguments below:
- While usability focuses on quantitative indicators such as task success rates, number of clicks and response time to evaluate efficiency and effectiveness, UX focuses on qualitative indicators such as customer satisfaction, and takes into account psychology, sociology, and anthropology.
- While UX focuses on emotions, usability focuses on logic.
- UX and usability have emerged as different disciplines because managing the emotional and logical aspects of design separately is a more effective method of creating user centered designs.

Assertion D – Usability is a subset of UX.

Usability is a subset of UX

Before reaching a conclusion, the term "UX" must clearly be defined. UX pioneers Don Norman and Jakob Nielsen define user experience as "encompassing all aspects of the end-user's interaction with the company, its services, and its products." According to this definition, in order to be able to discuss UX, there should be an interaction between the user and the product/service. But this experience should not be limited to the time span when the user uses or buys the product/service. Instead, UX should be thought of in a broader context. The experience should span from the time the user is aware of the product/service (attract) to:

- The time the user researches the product/service (engage)
- The time the user purchases or uses the product/service (transact)
- The time the user repurchases or reuses the product/service (retain)
- The time the user recommends the product/service to somebody else (grow)

Figure 11.1 User journey

The user experience should last until the user stops using or talking about the product/service. In other words, UX is the end-to-end experience that is created between the product/service and the user.

In order to evaluate the validity of the assertion that usability is a subset of UX (assertion d), consider the following hypothetical conversation between the user and the usability specialist:

Usability Specialist: *So tell me the characteristics of a successful product/service which creates a high-quality user experience.*

User: *Well, I think it is obvious. As long as the product/service meets my expectations and needs, then it is satisfactory.*

The words "expectations" and "needs" mentioned in the above conversation are the keywords for the analysis of the assertion. In business analysis terminology, user expectations and needs are represented by requirements, which are classified into two main categories:

- Functional requirements which define what the system is supposed to do
- Non-functional requirements which define how the system should work

The non-functional requirements can be classified into sub-categories such as:

- Usability
- Performance
- Security
- Reliability
- Interoperability
- Compatibility
- Maintainability

In the dialogue between the usability specialist and the user, the user mentions that she wants her expectations and needs (thus her requirements) to be met. Based on the requirement classification scheme defined above, the user wants her functional requirements and non-functional requirements (such as usability, performance, security, reliability, interoperability, compatibility and maintainability requirements) to be met. This list of requirements can even be extended to the physical, mental, emotional, and content requirements of the user.

As is obvious from the requirements list, the usability requirement is only one of the requirements of the user and is not enough, in and of itself, to create a high-quality UX. If this is the case, then why the current emphasis on the importance of usability? Much research has been conducted recently on the topic of usability, perhaps because it is the most visible aspect of the product/service to the user, as long as functionality is working properly. Without functionality, though, all other non-functional aspects of a product/service, even usability, become irrelevant. Therefore, in the case of a product's/service's providing the same working functionality as other products/services, a new approach is needed to differentiate the product/service from other products/services. The following case study will further illustrate the dilemma between functionality and usability:

Case A

Assume that a presentation is scheduled to be delivered in a hotel facility on the basement floor, with no access to sunlight. The presenter arrives at the hotel early to make sure that all equipment is set up properly. Since there is no light in the room, the presenter instinctively tries to hit the light switch upon entering but cannot find the switch. After stumbling in the dark, the presenter finally locates the switch and manages to turn on the lights.

Case B

Assume that a presenter arrives at the same dark hotel room and attempts to turn on the lights. On the first attempt, the presenter hits the switch, only to find that the lights are not working. She presses the switch a few more times, with no success. Finally, the presenter decides to call the hotel staff for help but is now running behind schedule.

One might assume that the dilemma posed in Case B is the more frustrating, since in the first case, the presenter is eventually able to turn on the lights. Though the room in Case A has usability problems (the switch is not conveniently located), at least the lights function properly. In the second case, however, although the switch is conveniently located, or usable, it is not working; the switch lacks functionality. Similarly, from a UX perspective, all non-functional requirements such as usability, performance, security, and reliability have no relevance without working functionality. Even in the case of working functionality, however, the ability of a product/service to satisfy only the user's usability requirements is not sufficient: other non-functional requirements of the user have to be met as well.

To sum up, in order to create a high-quality UX, a product/service must satisfy both the functional and non-functional requirements of its intended users. Skipping even one of the requirements may cause a defect in the UX. The correct answer to the chapter question, then, is assertion d: UX is a superset of usability.

Chapter 12

Usability Maturity Level

Question
Please rate the usability maturity level of your company.
(Lowest maturity 1, Highest maturity 5)

    a. 1
    b. 2
    c. 3
    d. 4
    e. 5

Usability Maturity Level

In order to limit the scope of the chapter question and focus on the IT industry, assume that one is working at a software development company and trying to rate her company's usability maturity level. Her detailed evaluation of the following aspects of the usability efforts in her company will help her calculate the maturity level of her company:

- Responsibility
- Timing
- Usability processes
- Usability testing
- User involvement
- Management attitude towards usability
- Interaction design
- User research

To elaborate the different aspects of usability efforts mentioned above, the professional working in a software development company will be asked a question for each of them. In each question, the usability maturity level of a software development company increases from option a to option e, where option a represents 1 point and option e represents 5 points. The arithmetic mean of points obtained from each question will reveal the usability maturity level of her company.

Responsibility

Who is responsible for user interface (UI) design in a software development company?

a. No one
b. Software developers
c. Business analysts
d. Graphic designers
e. Under the guidance of usability specialists, UIs are designed with the involvement of users, business analysts, software developers, graphic designers, interaction designers, information architects, usability testers, and user researchers.

With the increasing level of usability maturity from option a to option e, in this question, a reader may wonder why it is asserted that business analysts can design better user interfaces than software developers. The reason behind this assertion is neither personal nor related to the titles hereby used but instead implies that business analysts are closer to users than software developers. Because business analysts are in close contact with the end users during requirements elicitation sessions, it is easier for them to put themselves in the shoes of the users. By doing so, business analysts may translate users' needs into user interfaces more easily. In addition, while designing UIs, the software developer's focus may shift to system details whereas business analysts tend to focus on users.

The next option in the question is "graphic designers." Compared to business analysts, whose main responsibility is to elicit and model requirements (as their title indicates), the graphic designer's main responsibility is to design interfaces. Although user interfaces are the visualization of user requirements and can be constructed by business analysts, designing user interfaces requires design skills and special competencies.

The fifth and most mature option, option e, places emphasis on teamwork. Even a talented usability specialist cannot guarantee success on her own; the involvement of other project team members, especially that of users, is the key factor in successful user interface design. In this option, a usability specialist's guidance, rather than a graphic designer's, is important because "usability" is a broader term than "graphic design."

Timing
When is UI designed?
  a. At no specific time
  b. During coding
  c. Major interfaces during business analysis, others during coding
  d. During business analysis
  e. Starting from the project kick-off meeting and continuing to and beyond the software's release to the market

The first sign of a software development company's giving importance to usability is its shifting of efforts from development to UI design and the inclusion of these UI design efforts in its project plan. UI design is now part of the coding as well as the project plan, but is not sufficient in and of itself. UIs designed during coding may not accurately reflect the users' needs and expectations. UIs designed at this stage are more system-centric, more functionality-oriented, and difficult to change, since any change request requires changes in code.

In more mature software development companies, all UIs are designed during the business analysis phase. In some companies, only the major, key interfaces are designed during business analysis, while others are left to software developers.

Although designing UIs during the business analysis phase helps the company increase its usability maturity level and create more user-centric UIs, it is still not sufficient because the life of the UIs should span from the project kick-off meeting to and beyond the software's release to the market. UI design is neither a step nor a Gantt chart row in the project timeline but is rather an end-to-end process which should evolve iteratively over time. It involves a journey of continuously learning about one's users. UI design, therefore, should be seamlessly integrated into and parallel with the software development lifecycle.

Usability Processes
Which one of the following best describes the usability processes in a software development company?
   a. Usability processes do not exist
   b. Only graphic design processes exist
   c. There is a defined User Centered Design (UCD) process
   d. There is a defined UCD process whose effectiveness and efficiency is measured by using key performance indicators (KPIs) and critical success factors (CSFs)
   e. The UCD process is institutionalized, monitored, and continuously improved

In order to answer the question concerning usability processes, it is first necessary to define User Centered Design, or UCD:

"An approach or philosophy that emphasizes early and continuous involvement of users in the design and evaluation process." [UXPA Glossary]

UCD process should include but should not be limited to the following processes:

- User research
- User profiling
- Persona identification
- Scope definition
- Interaction design
- Information architecture development
- Interface design
- Navigation design
- Prototyping
- Graphic design
- Usability testing

Although the processes in the above list appear as discrete elements, they are iterative in practice and can overlap and interact in many ways.

According to the above definition of UCD, it is obvious that it is comprised of more than just graphic design, which may be regarded as only the tip of the iceberg. Without the building blocks of UCD listed above, even the use of elaborate, trendy graphic design elements do not help develop usable software.

Even with a well-functioning UCD process in place within a software development company, the UCD process should also be allowed to evolve, since users also evolve over time. New techniques, processes, and tools should therefore be adopted by the UCD process. This can only be realized if the effectiveness and efficiency of UCD processes are measured by key performance indicators (KPIs) and critical success factors (CSFs). These KPIs and CSFs are the gatekeepers which help prevent the UCD process from becoming outdated. The following are a few common KPIs and CSFs:

- Has user research been conducted?
- How many user research techniques are used?
- Have style guides been defined and used?
- How many personas have been defined?
- Has a mind-map for each persona been defined?
- How many secondary scenarios have been defined for each primary scenario during interaction design?

- How many participants per persona have attended usability tests?
- Have usability tests been conducted on prototypes?

Having a well-defined UCD process, as well as KPIs and CSFs, however, is still not sufficient in developing usable software. UCD processes and their KPIs and CSFs should be embraced, implemented, and continuously improved by every member of the project team–from the business unit to the business analyst, the software developer to the project manager, and the usability specialist to the software tester. By doing so, a self-evolving and institutionalized UCD can be achieved.

Usability Testing

When and how are usability tests conducted?
a. Usability tests are not conducted
b. Usability tests are conducted during user acceptance tests (UAT) by relying only on user observations of working interfaces
c. In addition to the usability tests conducted during UAT, usability specialists conduct heuristic evaluations on working interfaces
d. In addition to user observations and heuristic evaluations conducted on working interfaces, usability specialists also conduct heuristic evaluations on prototypes
e. In addition to user observations and heuristic evaluations conducted on working interfaces, both heuristic evaluations and user observations are conducted on prototypes

Those who are aware of static testing and its importance would probably agree that usability testing should begin as early as possible in SDLC. According to the ISTQB® Glossary, the definition of static testing is as follows:

"Testing of a software development artifact, e.g., requirements, design or code, without execution of these artifacts, e.g., reviews or static analysis."
[ISTQB® Glossary]

The same is true for usability testing as well. A usability tester does not have to wait until she has working interfaces in order to run usability tests. Heuristic evaluations and user observations can be conducted on prototypes such as sketches, mock-ups, and wire-frames. This type of usability testing, conducted iteratively during the design and prototyping stages to help guide (or "form") the design by identifying usability design defects, is called "formative usability testing." By conducting formative usability testing, a usability tester receives early feedback from users and locates usability design defects in the early stages of the SDLC, leading to cost savings. Compared to summative usability testing that is conducted after implementation in order to measure usability and identify problems in a completed component or system, formative usability testing is simpler, cheaper, and results in a higher return on investment.

A usability tester may wonder why project teams generally do not conduct formative usability tests. The answer is straightforward: first, project teams may not believe that they can gather enough information from a method that is considerably inexpensive; second, they may believe that they should wait until they have a better user interface before they test it.

User Involvement
When are users involved in usability processes?
  a.   Users are never involved in usability processes
  b.   User feedback about UI design is gathered only during user acceptance tests (UAT)
  c.   While developing working interfaces, users are partially involved in usability processes before UAT
  d.   Users are involved early in usability processes, starting from prototype development
  e.   Users are involved in usability processes by conducting user research, even before the project kick-off

The question of "if and when" to involve users in usability processes may seem surprising since the primary objective of project team members, after all, is to design usable software for users. It may seem obvious that users, therefore, should be involved at every stage in usability processes, but unfortunately, this does not always happen. Due to time and budget constraints, or to their unwillingness to go to the user location, project team members generally work from behind a desk rather than venturing out into the field to speak directly with users. In this case a gap occurs between designer's and user's mental models where the designer assumes that the user will use the software in the way the designer envisions. However, in reality, the user's perception of the software may differ significantly from the designer's perception, thus resulting in dissatisfaction with the implemented software. The only way to resolve this problem is to involve users in every stage of the usability processes, starting even before the project commences by conducting user research.

Management Attitude Towards Usability

What is management's attitude towards usability?

a. Management is unaware of the importance of usability
b. Management believes that usability is unnecessary
c. Management considers investing in usability
d. Management believes that usability is important
e. Management collaborates with usability teams

Because usability is a new concept, management may have varying attitudes towards it. Listed below are the maturity levels of management's attitude towards usability, progressing from the lowest to the highest levels:

a. Unaware of the importance of usability: Management may think that usability only interests graphic designers. Management has no room for usability in its agenda.
b. Thinks that usability is unnecessary: Management may be misled in thinking that investing in usability is a waste of time and may choose instead to invest in new features and functionality. Management relies on its own experience when making usability decisions.
c. Considers investing in usability: Management may consider allocating a budget for usability while still viewing it as a nice-to-have item.
d. Thinks that usability is important: Management may allocate a budget for usability, but only for high priority projects.
e. Collaborates with usability teams: Management may see usability as a kind of culture in that it is integrated into every project and must be the responsibility of everyone, including management, itself. Management promotes usability metrics as part of the company's strategic scorecard and creates a usability vision.

Interaction Design

How is the interaction design process handled in a company?

    a. An interaction design process does not exist

    b. The interaction design process is considered equivalent to graphic design

    c. The interaction design process is considered equivalent to interface design

    d. The interaction design process is considered part of the business analysis process

    e. The interaction design process is considered as a separate discipline, blending business processes and users' ergonomic needs

Interaction design is usually confused with interface and graphic design. Although interaction design contains the word "design", it is more related to business analysis than to interface and graphic design. According to Interaction Design Association (IxDA), the definition of interaction design is as follows:

The discipline of Interaction Design (IxD) defines the structure and behavior of interactive systems. Interaction Designers strive to create meaningful relationships between people and the products and services that they use, from computers to mobile devices to appliances and beyond. [IxDA]

So, interaction design can be summed as the act of designing process flow between the user and the software from the user's point of view. For example, assume that the interaction between a user and an online email service is being designed. The interaction design, and thus the process flow of the login use case of this online email service, may appear as follows:

Login Use Case	
Step 1	User enters her username in a text box
Step 2	User enters her password in a text box
Step 3	User clicks "Login" button
Step 4	If username and password combination is valid, then user sees her inbox. If not valid, user sees an error message.

As seen in the steps of login use case, the subjects of each sentence are "user" because in interaction design the process flow should be designed from the user's point of view.

Another confusing term for many project members is interface design, or the method of interaction between the user and the software. In the login use case, text boxes and a button form the interface and thus the interaction medium between the user and the software. Instead of using text boxes and a button, however, the same interaction may be achieved by implementing a voice recognition feature. By using voice recognition as the interaction medium for the login use case, the process flow and thus the interaction design remain the same, even though the interface design has changed. In usability projects, interface design is generally followed by graphic design, at which stage font type and size, as well as color and the image of the design elements are determined.

In sum, interaction design can be defined as a separate discipline which blends business processes and users' ergonomic needs, and lays the groundwork for interface and graphic design.

User Research
How is user research carried out in a software development company?
    a. User research is never conducted
    b. User research is carried out through interviews with internal representatives
    c. User research is carried out through interviews with random users
    d. User research is carried out through interviews and focus groups with users from selected personas
    e. User research is carried out not only through interviews and focus groups with users from selected personas, but also through ethnographic research techniques

The formula for developing usable software is simple: the better user needs are understood, the more usable the software will be. Therefore, users should be systematically consulted at every stage of usability processes. Prospective users should be identified and classified according to their behaviors to create a fictitious person who represents their behaviors, called a persona. While creating a persona rather than only consulting proxies such as business unit representatives, project team members should directly consult with end users and invite them to interviews, focus groups, and workshops. Consulting with end users may even be taken to the next level through systematic and nonintrusive observations of them in their natural context, such as in their homes, offices, or workplaces. This type of ethnographic research would allow user behavior to be observed on the users' terms, rather than on those of the observer, so that the reality of users' lives may be better understood.

Chapter 13

Misconceptions About Usability

Question
Which of the statements below regarding usability is/are false?

a. Usability tests should not be conducted until working user interfaces and graphic designs are developed
b. The best method of user segmentation is to categorize users according to their demographic information such as age, income level, computer literacy, and gender
c. Only usability specialists should be responsible for usability
d. Understanding users and their needs is the only requirement needed to develop usable software
e. The root cause of a usability problem may be the incompetence of the users
f. All of the above
g. None of the above

Misconceptions About Usability

Before arriving at a conclusion to the chapter question, each assertion will be examined in detail.

Assertion a: Usability tests should not be conducted until working user interfaces and graphic designs are developed.

If a company chose a waterfall software development model as its software development lifecycle (SDLC) methodology, then this assertion may seem to be a valid position. Below are the main phases in the waterfall model:

Figure 13.1 Waterfall software development model

According to the waterfall model, software tests, including usability tests, are conducted on working user interfaces at the end of a project. However, this method is generally not successful. Because fixing a bug during later phases of a project is difficult and costly, many project teams now realize that tests should be conducted parallel to the SDLC, starting with the requirement analysis phase. This paradigm shift in the perception of testing has also triggered a paradigm shift in usability testing; that is, usability tests should be conducted as early as possible.

Any project team member may wonder how usability tests can be conducted without first having working user interfaces. In order to clarify this issue, a modified version of the existing UX framework from Jesse James Garret's *Elements of User Experience* is proposed to help project team members understand how to conduct usability testing on software starting from ideation stage through to the release of the software:

119

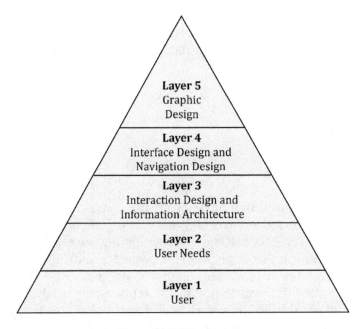

Figure 13.2 UX Framework

Using the above framework, the following table identifies the types of usability tests which might be conducted at each layer:

Layer Name	Purpose of the layer	Usability tests that could be conducted at this layer
User	To identify the demographic information and behavior of the software's intended users	Any kind of user analysis technique such as brainstorming, focus group, interview, job shadowing, usage pattern tracking, ethnographic study, or any user research technique could be used at this layer. Usage of these techniques would allow project team members not only to better understand the users but also to test their understanding of the users.
User needs	To identify the functional, non-functional, emotional, and content requirements of the software's intended users.	Use case modeling and mind mapping techniques could be used to conduct usability testing at this layer.
Interaction design and information architecture	Interaction design: *"to define the structure and behavior of interactive systems."* [IxDA] Information architecture: *"to arrange the parts of something to be understandable."* [IAI]	In interaction design, process flow diagrams could be used, and in information architecture, card sorting and tree testing techniques could be used to conduct usability testing at this layer.
Interface design and navigation design	Interface design: *"to arrange interface elements to enable users to interact with the functionality of the system."* [Garret 2011] Navigation design: *"to arrange a set of screen elements that allow the user to move through the information architecture."* [Garret 2011]	The below techniques could be used to conduct usability testing on low-fidelity prototypes such as paper prototypes and wireframes at this layer: • 5-second tests • Click tests • A/B tests • Eye tracking • Surveys • Task analysis • Timing • Video recording • Thinking aloud • Retrospective thinking aloud
Graphic design	To define the look and feel of the design, such as color, font types, font sizes, image, sound, and video.	The below techniques could be used to conduct usability testing on high-fidelity prototypes or working interfaces at this layer: • 5-second tests • Click tests • A/B tests • Eye tracking • Surveys • Task analysis • Logging • Timing • Video recording • Thinking aloud • Retrospective thinking aloud

Table 13.1 Different layers of UX framework and their related usability tests

According to the UX framework, usability tests can be conducted at any layer (even at the user layer), even if the graphic designs are not completed until the graphic design layer. In the case that working interfaces are needed in order to conduct usability tests, they may be fabricated by using paper prototypes and prototyping tools. Because there is no need to wait for graphic designs and coded interfaces in order to conduct usability tests, the assertion that "usability tests should not be conducted until working user interfaces and graphic designs are developed" is false.

The earlier usability tests are conducted, the more insight will be gained about users and designs. Conducting usability tests during the early phases of the SDLC can even help project team members revise their software's strategy and objectives. Usability tests conducted in the late phases of the SDLC, however, have only minor impacts on the design. Unfortunately, it is common to hear questions similar to the ones below within companies whose usability maturity levels are low and whose usability tests are conducted during the later stages of the SDLC:

Question 1: Should the reporting feature button be blue or red in color?
Answer 1: Since the company's corporate colors include blue, the button should be blue in color.

Question 2: Should the reporting feature button be placed on the left-hand side of the page layout, or the right-hand side?
Answer 2: Since users are accustomed to seeing buttons on the right-hand side of the page layout, the button should remain on the right-hand side.

Although the answers to the above questions may initially seem correct, they are not. The reason for this is that the first question addresses the fifth layer (the graphic design layer), while the second question addresses the fourth layer (the interface design layer). Before questioning user experience at these higher layers, user experience should first be questioned at the lower layers, as shown in the following:

Question 3: Do users really require the functionality associated with the button mentioned in the above questions?

If the answer to the Question 3 is "no", then the first two questions are irrelevant. The third question requires a more in-depth reasoning that appears in the second layer (user needs), and is therefore the more appropriate question. In order to be able to ask the right questions, project team members should approach user experience and usability from a broader perspective and begin conducting usability tests immediately, even at the project's kick-off stage. Otherwise, project team members may fall into the trap of seeking the right answers to the wrong questions, as is the case in the first and second questions mentioned above.

Assertion b: The best method of user segmentation is to categorize users according to their demographic information such as age, income level, computer literacy, and gender.

The following are common demographic survey questions typically asked:
- What is your age?
- What is your income level?
- How computer literate are you?
- Do you own a smart phone?

From the answers given to the above questions, it would be almost impossible to design a web page that successfully targeted intended users. The following example shall illustrate why this is the case:

Assume that a project team has been assigned to develop microsites for different user segments of a brand new toothbrush. Which of the following user segmentation approaches would best help achieve usable microsites?

Approach A – Segmenting users according to their age:
- Ages 10 - 18
- Ages 19 - 35
- Ages 36 - 50
- Ages 50+

Approach B – Segmenting users according to their brushing habits:
- Once a day
- Twice a day

123

- Three times a day
- Irregularly

The main difference between the above approaches is that approach A is a simpler way of segmenting users. Approach B, on the other hand, is a meta-segmentation of the segment presented in Approach A.

For example, users who brush twice a day might belong to any age range, as brushing behavior is independent of age. The possible relationship between brushing behavior and age can be depicted as follows:

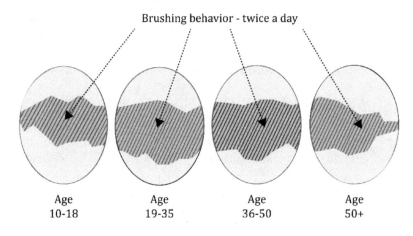

Figure 13.3 The possible relationship between brushing behavior and age

Since microsites are developed for users, rather than for machines, user behavior is the key in achieving usable microsites. Focusing primarily on users' demographic information such as age will only provide project team members with a shallow insight, which is insufficient when developing usable microsites. As a result, assertion b that "the best method of user segmentation is to categorize users according to their demographic information such as age, income level, computer literacy, and gender" is false.

Behavior-based segmentations might be further extended to include the definition of personas representing the product's/service's ideal examples of target users. Personas represent who the users are, which activities they wish to perform, and why they might use the product or service. The following is a sample persona created for a toothbrush company:

Mary 	"Brushing is an important part of my daily routine"
Demographic Info **Age:** 25 – 35 **Occupation:** HR Specialist **Marital Status:** Married with one child **Income:** > 80,000 USD **Interest:** Anti-aging diets, reading, traveling **Technical profile:** Proficient with technology	**Mary's brushing behavior** 1. Mary is very health conscious and considers brushing an important part of her daily routine 2. Mary brushes her teeth upon waking up in the morning 3. After breakfast, Mary never forgets to floss 4. Mary brings her toothbrush and toothpaste to work every day 5. Even though Mary has a very busy work schedule, she always makes time to floss and brush her teeth after lunch 6. At night, Mary never goes to bed without flossing and brushing her teeth

Identifying a persona is not easy, as it requires that users be observed in their natural context such as in their homes, offices, or workplaces. Ideally, data gathered during these observations should be analyzed, and patterns about user behavior identified, with the observer taking on the role of sociologist.

Assertion c: Only usability specialists should be responsible for usability.

Imagine a project for which coding, testing and primitive user interfaces are almost complete, with only two weeks remaining before its release. The conversation below takes place between the project manager and usability specialists:

Project manager: *"Everything is ready except for usable user interfaces. You have two weeks to design usable and trendy user interfaces, which should not be too difficult."*

It is obvious from the above comment that the project manager in this example is not fully aware of the definition of usability, the importance of early involvement of usability specialists, and the need for teamwork and cooperation between project team members in a successful usability initiative. The only improvement that can be achieved within a tight deadline at the end of a project is a few minor changes to the graphic design.

Contrary to the project manager's assignment of responsibility only to usability specialists to create usable user interfaces, in practice, usability is not only the responsibility of usability specialists but also the responsibility of every member of the project team–from the business unit to business analysts, software developers, graphic designers, software testers, and project managers. The varying responsibilities of usability tasks can be delegated to different members of a project by using a RACI matrix for usability tasks. A RACI matrix may be defined as follows:

- R = Responsible for doing the work
- A = Accountable to the decision maker
- C = Consulted prior to the completion of the work
- I = Informed after the work is complete

By using the RACI matrix, the division of usability tasks among project members can be depicted as follows:

Usability Task	Responsible	Accountable	Consulted	Informed
Identify Personas	Usability Specialist	Usability Team Leader	Business Analyst	Project Manager
Elicit User Requirements	Business Analysts	Business Analyst Team Leader		Usability Specialist
Design Graphics and Visuals	Graphic Designer	Usability Specialist	Business Analyst	Usability Team Leader / Project Manager
Conduct Usability Tests	Users / Business Units	Usability Specialist / Usability Tester		Usability Team Leader /Project Manager / Test Manager

Table 13.2 The division of usability tasks among project members in a RACI matrix

As illustrated in the above RACI matrix, every project team member plays a role in the process of developing usable software. Therefore, all project team members, including users, should possess a basic understanding of usability and its principles. Usability should be perceived as an integral part of the culture of a company, not as the sole responsibility of usability specialists. As a result, assertion c that "only usability specialists should be responsible for usability" is false.

Assertion d: Understanding users and their needs is the only requirement needed to develop usable software.

The missing element in the above assertion is the context of use of the product/service. Context may be defined as the situation in which something happens; the group of conditions that exist where and when something happens. Situation and conditions of use of the product/service play an important role in identifying users' perceptions of usability. Under disruptive conditions, user satisfaction is badly affected. Successful software, therefore, should be designed according to such conditions. Matching users to their needs, context of use, and the intended software will result in a greater chance of achieving usable software. Usability functions at its best, therefore, when it considers the intersection of users, their needs, and their context of use.

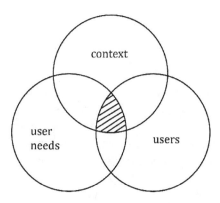

Figure 13.4 The intersection of users, their needs and their context of use

The following is a real world example of the importance of context:

Case Study
Usability Testing of a Shipping Company's Handheld Devices

A software test team is in charge of the usability testing of a shipping company's new handheld devices, which feature enhanced memory capabilities, new functionalities, and a high-speed wireless connection. In order to conduct usability tests, the shipping company's staff is invited to the usability lab and given various tasks. During the usability tests, minor usability defects are found. Having corrected these defects, the devices are made ready for release. Because ground times and lead times play an important role in a logistic company's ability to gain a competitive advantage, usability of these handheld devices is vital, and the software test team dedicates a considerable amount of time and effort to designing and performing such usability tests. In the end, a go-live decision is made, and the project team anticipates success.

Unexpectedly, there is a 30% increase in lead and ground times, resulting in hundreds of thousands of dollars of additional costs. The root cause behind the increase in lead and ground times is misuse of the new handheld devices. Staff members had been mistakenly pressing the wrong buttons. The usability testing team is confused since everything appeared to be working properly during the usability tests and the shipping company's staff had achieved a success rate of almost 95% in the usability test tasks given. In order to find the root cause behind the misuse of the new handheld devices, the test team decides to observe the staff in their working environment. Surprisingly, there is a slight difference in the use of the handheld devices between the usability lab and the real working environment— the staff had been using the handheld devices while wearing gloves to hold steel ropes. Because the buttons on the new handheld devices are smaller than those on the older ones, it is difficult for the staff to press the buttons with their gloved hands, causing them to enter the wrong inputs.

Although conditions, with the exception of the gloved hands, were the same in both the test and the real work environment, a slight change in the context of use resulted in a major difference in the users' capability to use the handset. This example reinforces the importance of context in usability. Special attention, therefore, should be paid to context and the intersection of users, their needs, and their context of use. As a result, assertion d that "understanding users and their needs is the only requirement needed to develop usable software" is false.

Assertion e: The root cause of a usability problem may be the incompetence of the users.

During usability testing projects, one may encounter conversations similar to the one below:

Client Employee: Why is the test participant struggling so much to find the "About Us" item in the menu? It seems so obvious. Our real users should easily be able to find that. Who is this user?

Usability Specialist: She represents your persona named "Mary" in terms of both her behavior patterns and demographic information. Your team found her from your customer database for user observation sessions. We think she is a perfect fit with your persona.

Client Employee: Hmm, no, our users should be more capable.

It may be difficult for client employees to accept that a prospective user might struggle with, or even criticize their software. Such criticism may upset or even offend client employees. When confronted with such a conflict, client employees may rush to blame the counter party, even though the user may express a valid concern with the usability of the company's software. Instead of blaming or ignoring the user, client employees must be able to take user feedback into account, even when the user may seem to be struggling with the simplest of tasks. Furthermore, client employees must be open to question both themselves and the software in the effort to make it more usable. Even though the company's users may be very capable, real world conditions and the hassles of daily life may produce unexpected results.

In order to develop usable software, users should be assumed as lazy and, due to their daily hassle, as confused, and as Steve Krug [2000] mentions in his book *Don't Make Me Think*, users should be prevented from thinking. A usability specialist may wonder why Krug uses the word "thinking" in the title of the book instead of "going crazy," "getting angry" or "being frustrated". Most probably, Steve Krug's reasoning behind the title of the book is that before going crazy, getting angry, or being frustrated, people first tend to think. Usable software requires that users be able to intuitively find what they are looking for, without having to think too much.

Based on the above analysis, assertion e that "the root cause of a usability problem may be the incompetence of the users" is also false. Thus, all the assertions in the chapter question are false.

Chapter 14

Usability Testing Versus User Acceptance Testing: Are They the Same?

Question

Which one of the online banking test scenarios below can be considered an example of user acceptance testing?

a	**Test Case A** Wire transfer 100 USD from XXX account to YYY account within the same bank.
	Expected Result XXX account should be debited 100 USD, and YYY account should be credited 100 USD.
b	**Test Case B** Check how many seconds it takes to transfer the funds.
	Expected Result Funds should be transferred within 1 second, at most.
c	**Test Case C** How likely is it that you would recommend the wire transfer feature to a friend or colleague?
	Expected Result Average net promoter score (NPS) of at least 9 points over 10 points.
d	Test Cases A, B, and C are all examples of user acceptance testing.
e	Test Cases A, B, and C are examples of different test types and can be run at the user acceptance test level.

Usability Testing Versus User Acceptance Testing: Are They the Same?

Usability testing and user acceptance testing are not the same; they address different aspects of software testing. The difference between usability testing and user acceptance testing might be illustrated with an analogy between software testing and the design of a restaurant menu. In order to describe a particular dish, any one of the categorizations below or their combinations can be used:

    a.   The course of the dish: appetizer, soup, main dish, dessert, etc.

    b.   The taste profile of the dish: spicy, sour, sweet, etc.

A meal might be described as both a main dish and as a spicy dish, such as "Chinese roast duck with spicy duck sauce," or a dish might be described as both a dessert and as a sour dish, such as "sour cream cookies." The same is true for software testing. In order to accurately describe software tests, at least two aspects of software testing should be identified—test levels and test types. The following figure illustrates the relationship between these two aspects of software testing:

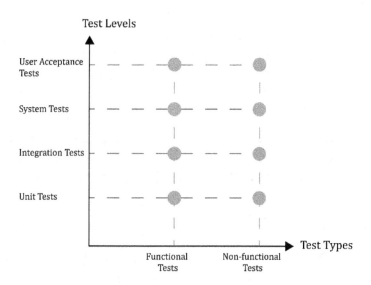

Figure 14.1 Test levels and test types

Test Levels

When test levels are listed from bottom to top, according to their level of detail, the list starts with unit tests and continues with integration tests, system tests, and finally user acceptance tests.

Unit Tests

Unit tests are generally conducted by software developers in order to verify the functions, modules, or classes of the software. Bugs found at this stage are typically fixed as soon as they are found, without formally recording them into the bug tracking system.

Integration Tests

Successfully passed or waived unit tests are followed by integration tests, where the interfaces between components or component's interactions with different parts of a system are tested.

System Tests

Having successfully completed integration tests, the system is ready to be tested as a whole. The only unfinished part may be its user interface. At this level, the system might be compared to a desktop computer without its case. Because there is no case covering the computer's components, the cables connecting its components, as well as the dust that has collected inside the computer, are all visible, and the noise of the fan is heard more audibly. At this stage, the computer may not look complete, but this does not affect the functioning of the computer, and it can still be tested from end-to-end.

User Acceptance Tests

Imagine that system tests for the computer have successfully been completed, and it is now ready to be covered with its case and shipped to end-customers. But before being released to the market, it should first be confirmed that the desktop computer is operating in a manner suited to real-world circumstances and usage. Tests conducted for this purpose by end-users include user requirements, use cases, and business processes as inputs and are called "user acceptance tests." Users are responsible for user acceptance tests, but other stakeholders may be involved, as well. High success rates of tests at this level will ensure that the product is ready to be shipped.

To wrap up, test level is an important aspect of software testing and should be clearly indicated when describing a particular test. In this chapter, test levels are defined from bottom to top, according to their level of detail, which means that an upper-level test may include some test cases belonging to the lower levels. For example, a system test case may cover some of the test cases carried out at the integration and unit levels.

Test Types

Functional Tests

Functional testing is the testing of what the system is supposed to do and is based on functions and features. Functional tests can be performed at all levels. For example, in the case of a credit card system, the following table shows the functional test cases that can be carried out at each test level:

Test Level – Test Type	Test Case
Unit Level – Functional Test	Testing the functionality of an algorithm used for encrypting a 16-digit credit card number in order to evaluate whether it is successfully encrypting the credit card number
Integration Level – Functional Test	Testing the interaction between the encryption feature and account feature of the credit card system in order to evaluate whether they are communicating correctly with valid inputs and outputs
System Level – Functional Test	Testing the credit card system by using an SQL query in order to evaluate whether it is authorizing a valid credit card
User Acceptance Level – Functional Test	Requiring users to test the credit card system through a graphical user interface in order to evaluate whether it is authorizing a valid credit card

Option a presented in the chapter question is an example of a functional test at the user acceptance level:

Test Case A
Wire transfer 100 USD from XXX account to YYY account within the same bank
Expected Result
XXX account should be debited 100 USD, and YYY account should be credited 100 USD

Non-functional Tests

Non-functional tests evaluate the service levels related to a function or feature. Non-functional testing is the testing of how the system should work. Performance, usability, reliability, and compatibility are all examples of service level categories from which non-functional tests can be derived. Non-functional tests can be performed at all levels as well. The case of the credit card system further illustrates how non-functional tests might be carried out:

Test Levels – Test Types	Test
Unit Level – Performance Test	Testing the performance of an encryption algorithm in order to evaluate whether it is encrypting the credit card number in under 1 second
Integration Level – Performance Test	Testing the speed of interaction between encryption and account features in order to evaluate whether they are communicating in less than 10 milliseconds
System Level – Performance Test	Testing the performance of the credit card system by using an SQL query in order to evaluate whether it is authorizing a valid credit card in under 1 second
User Acceptance Level – Performance Test	Requiring users to test the performance of a credit card system through a user interface in order to evaluate whether its response time for authorizing a valid credit card is less than 1 second.

Options b and c of the chapter question are both examples of non-functional tests at the user acceptance level. While option b is a performance test at the user acceptance level, option c is a usability test at the user acceptance level.

Test Case B
Check how many seconds it takes to transfer the funds
Expected Result
Funds should be transferred within 1 second, at most

Test Case C
How likely is it that you would recommend the wire transfer feature to a friend or colleague?
Expected Result
Average net promoter score (NPS) of at least 9 points over 10 points.

To sum up, test levels and test types can be compared to the different ways in which a dish might be described, such as the course or the taste profiles of the dish. When describing a meal, using only one category of description is generally not sufficient. The same is true for tests, as well. Since all test types can be performed at all test levels, it would be more accurate to identify at least two aspects of software testing (such as a functional test case at the user acceptance level, or a performance test case at the unit level) when describing a test.

After completing analysis of test levels and test types, a software tester may wonder to which axis black-box techniques such as equivalence partitioning and boundary value analysis and white-box techniques such as statement coverage and decision coverage belong. Because black-box and white-box techniques are distinctly different than test levels and test types, they should therefore be treated separately. In order to position these techniques in the realm of software testing, another axis should be drawn (such as axis Z) to complement the test level and test type axes. This means that black-box and white-box techniques can be used at any test level for any test type. Test techniques may be seen as another category of description in the restaurant menu analogy (e.g., the way in which the dish is served, such as hot or cold).

Concluding Chapter

Chapter 15

Who Is to Blame for Failed Information Technology (IT) Projects?

Question

According to extensive research conducted in the IT field, most IT projects are either cancelled, delivered over budget, delivered late, or unsuccessful, which means that IT projects generally fail to meet their objectives. Who, then, is to blame for failed IT projects?

    a.   The business unit
    b.   The business analyst
    c.   The system analyst
    d.   The software developer
    e.   The software test engineer
    f.   The project manager
    g.   The usability specialist
    h.   All of the above
    i.   None of the above

Hint: Assume that a project team has adopted the waterfall methodology. The relationship between the business unit and the project team is depicted below:

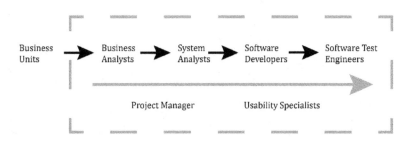

Figure 15.1 Roles in waterfall software development model

Who Is to Blame for Failed Information Technology (IT) Projects?

Assertion a: The guilty party is the business unit

Those who believe that the business unit is to blame for failed IT projects may express the following judgments and evidence-based arguments:

- Business units do not know what they want. Even though business units may seem sure of their needs, they are not able to express them clearly.
- When business analysts invite business units to requirements elicitation sessions in order to listen their needs, business units often ignore these invitations, using their busy schedules as an excuse. Despite their unwillingness to take part in requirements elicitation efforts, business units still demand that their needs be satisfied accurately.
- Business units do not prioritize their needs; all needs appear to be urgent and hold high priority.
- Once the project team meets the business units' needs, business units may claim that a particular feature was not included, even though it was never before mentioned.
- Business units believe that they are the profit centers of their company and that their company has no value without their presence; they are overly confident.
- Business units view the project team as their service provider rather than their business partner; they are very demanding.
- Business units assume that the project team has unlimited resources, time, and budgets. Business units are not aware of the project team's limitations and the infeasibility of their demands.

Assertion b: The guilty party is the business analyst

Those who believe that the business analyst is to blame for failed IT projects may express the following judgments and evidence-based arguments:

- Business analysts cannot think like the business.

- Business analysts agree to all of the business units' demands without evaluating the demands' relevance to the company's goals. Business analysts cannot see the big picture; they lack strategic thinking skills.
- Business analysts are not aware of the technical feasibility of the solutions which might meet the business units' needs. They do not understand the limitations of the current system.
- Business analysts with a software development background mostly focus on system requirements or the solution itself, without understanding the user and the business implications of the need.
- Business analysts are not able to successfully manage the scope of the project. They tend to accept change requests without first questioning their necessity or impact.
- As business analysts do not use a traceability matrix, their evaluation of the business units' change requests is unjustified.
- Because business analysts cannot put themselves into the users' shoes, they are not aware of the users' real needs and priorities. Instead of focusing on must-have needs, therefore, business analysts tend to focus on nice-to-have needs.
- Business analysts' deficiency in project stakeholder identification and management skills leads to missing project stakeholders or requirements.
- The requirements business analysts gather are generally very vague. A requirement such as "a transaction should work quickly" is not clear. Business analysts must specify exact criteria: does "quickly" mean 5 seconds, 1 second, or 1 millisecond?

Assertion c: The guilty party is the system analyst

Those who believe that the system analyst is to blame for failed IT projects may express the following judgments and evidence-based arguments:
- The fact that system analysts work closely with software developers causes them to neglect the needs of business analysts and business units.

- System analysts are not able to successfully associate functional and non-functional requirements with system requirements.
- Even within the scope of the same project, system analysts sometimes use the business process approach and at other times may use the object-oriented approach to model system requirements; system analysts are not consistent.
- Without conducting adequate research and applying sufficient effort, system analysts may easily reject the business analysts' demands by claiming that they are technologically infeasible.

Assertion d: The guilty party is the software developer

Those who believe that the software developer is to blame for failed IT projects may express the following judgments and evidence-based arguments:
- Software developers primarily consider the technical side of the need rather than the user and her needs.
- Functionality is the only requirement that software developers take into consideration. Software developers do not fully understand usability, performance, and other non-functional requirements.
- While trying to arrive at the optimal solution, software developers make features more complex and confusing; they cannot arrive at a simple solution.
- Software developers are always reinventing the wheel and do not consider the reusability and the modularity of the features they develop.
- Software developers lack time management, resource management, and even basic project management skills.
- Software developers are continually occupied and therefore tend to postpone the business analysts' requests.
- Software developers interpret analysis and design documents from their own point of view rather than from the user's point of view and therefore tend to prioritize their own needs over those of the users.
- Software developers assume that quality is primarily the responsibility of the software testing team and do not properly conduct peer reviews or unit testing of their own work products.

Assertion e: The guilty party is the software test engineer

Those who believe that the software test engineer is to blame for failed IT projects may express the following judgments and evidence-based arguments:

- Software test engineers do not allocate enough time to properly conduct software testing because they lack time management skills.
- Although software test engineers run extensive tests, they are incapable of producing high-quality software.
- Software test engineers acquire modern and costly testing tools which do not necessarily result in better or more time-efficient testing results.
- Although business analysts provide software test engineers with detailed requirements, the test engineers still lack the necessary knowledge concerning writing test cases from these detailed requirements.
- Software test engineers generally report major bugs at the last minute, resulting in a delay in the release of the software.
- Software test engineers do not track the bugs they report; their bug reports are vague, and the bugs reported are not reproducible.

Assertion f: The guilty party is the project manager

Those who believe that the project manager is to blame for failed IT projects may express the following judgments and evidence-based arguments:

- The only deliverable project managers consider important is the project progress report. Project managers tend to question deadlines and Gantt charts, but not the product itself, as they do not fully understand the user, her needs, business domain, and technical limitations.
- Project managers do not take an active role in removing project blockages.
- The project managers' close ties to upper management and business units cause them to neglect the problems of other project team members.
- Because project managers possess limited knowledge of techniques and methodologies in software analysis, design,

development, and testing, they resort to delegating work in these disciplines to other project team members.

Assertion g: The guilty party is the usability specialist

Those who believe that the usability specialist is to blame for failed IT projects may express the following judgments and evidence-based arguments:

- Usability specialists do not adequately involve the users in the usability processes.
- Usability specialists tend to consult with user representatives or business units instead of consulting with the end users.
- Usability specialists do not conduct field studies.
- Usability specialists begin the usability processes without first conducting adequate user research.
- Usability specialists lack knowledge of UX design techniques.
- Usability specialists postpone usability testing until the end of the project.
- Usability specialists' user segmentations are mostly demographic and do not consider user behavior.

The tendency to pinpoint a guilty party for failed IT projects may result in confusion, as reasonable arguments might be made on behalf of both parties, depending on one's perspective. Folktales present many similar examples of this kind. The following is a well-known folktale from the Indian subcontinent which illustrates this dilemma:

The Elephant and the Blind Men

Once, an elephant appeared in a village for the very first time. Having never before encountered an elephant, six blind men in the village touched the elephant in an attempt to determine what it was.

The first blind man touched its long tail and said, "oh, it feels like a snake."

The second blind man touched its huge body and claimed that the elephant must be a wall.

The third blind man touched its wide ears and so believed that the elephant was a fan.

The fourth blind man touched its trunk and thought that the elephant was a large tree branch.

The fifth blind man touched its tusk and was sure that the elephant was a solid pipe.

The sixth blind man touched its leg and believed the elephant to be a pillar.

From the limited perspective of these six blind men, each is correct. The same can be said for the accused suspects of failed IT projects. Although the suspects may seem guilty in the eyes of the accusers, each accused party may make reasonable arguments justifying their innocence. Both parties, depending on perspective, may be correct. If this is the case, then, who is really to blame for failed IT projects? The answer is no one and everyone, as each project team member will approach the problem from her own perspective.

Each project team member may believe that her methods, priorities, and approaches are best for any given project; no project team member sets out to intentionally harm her company or the project. The main reason behind failed projects, then, is that project team members are unable to effectively communicate with each other because they cannot see beyond their own perspectives. Although this problem seems daunting, it may be easily overcome by working together to better understand the project goals and the viewpoints of others, and by prioritizing project goals over individual or departmental ones. Clearly, the success of IT projects requires that all project team members and business units be on the same page. The following are recommended actions for business units and individual project team members:

Recommended Actions for Business Units
- Before submitting new demands, business units should keep the bigger picture in mind by evaluating the importance of each demand and rejecting those that do not align with the company's overall strategy.
- Business units should prioritize their needs.

- Business units should evaluate the business impacts of their needs.
- Business units should outline and define their needs clearly so that they are not misunderstood by other project team members.
- When defining their needs, business units should use precise language instead of vague, ambiguous adjectives such as "fast," "user-friendly," or "reliable".

Recommended Actions for Business Analysts
- Business analysts should seek answers to the following questions:
  - What is the system supposed to do? (functional requirements)
  - How should the system work? (non-functional requirements)
- In addition to a project plan, there should be a complementary business analysis plan in place. Business analysts should distribute the business analysis plan to business units and other project team members in advance.
- Business analysts should be capable of deciding when and where to employ which business analysis techniques.
- Business analysts should focus on the identification of requirements from the user's point of view rather than from the system's point of view.
- When documenting requirements, business analysts should categorize them according to their type, such as business, user, functional, or non-functional.
- Business analysts should assign IDs to requirements to ensure that they are traceable.
- Business analysts should document requirements in a clear, correct, and consistent manner.
- Business analysts should conduct peer reviews for requirements.
- In order to avoid vague requirements, business analysts should ensure that test cases are written based on the requirements gathered. If the requirement is not testable, then it is not a precise requirement.
- Business analysts should keep the track of requirements by using traceability matrices.

Recommended Actions for System Analysts
- System analysts should be capable of translating the business units' needs identified by business analysts into solutions.
- System analysts should seek an answer to the following question:
  - How does the system do what it is supposed to do? (system requirements)
- System analysts should associate each written system requirement with a corresponding functional or non-functional requirement.
- System analysts should select their system requirement modeling approach based on the programming language which will be used. For example, for object-oriented programming languages, an object-oriented modeling approach should be selected.
- System analysts should provide solid justification for any rejection of the business unit's demands.

Recommended Actions for Software Developers
- When working with other project team members, software developers should avoid using technical or obscure terminology.
- Software developers should trace requirements coverage by associating written code to the related requirement.
- Software developers should code only what is required, rather than what they believe will be required.
- When software developers are unsure of the meaning of the requirements to be coded, they should avoid making assumptions and instead ask business analysts, system analysts, or business units for clarification.
- Software developers should be trained in business analysis and software testing skills.

Recommended Actions for Software Test Engineers
- Software test engineers should be involved in the project, beginning from the kick-off meeting, and should be regularly informed during all stages of the project.
- Software test engineers should not be limited to dynamic testing but should also conduct static testing.

- Software test engineers should keep track of requirements coverage and code coverage when writing test cases.
- Software test engineers' bug reports should be detailed enough and should have necessary descriptions and screenshots.
- Software test engineers should maintain a constructive attitude towards software developers.
- Software test engineers should divert their limited resources and time to risky parts of the software by using risk-based testing techniques; this approach will ensure effectiveness and efficiency.
- Software test engineers' test cases should be clear and easy to understand.
- Software test engineers should not be entirely dependent on test automation but should utilize testing tools when needed, and test manually for things not suitable for automation.

Recommended Actions for Project Managers
- Project managers should allocate time for each project team member.
- Project managers should allocate more time to understand the project's dynamics and the project's domain.
- Project managers should focus on achieving a working product rather than producing excessive or unnecessary paperwork and documentation.
- Project managers should encourage all project stakeholders to be involved in the project.

Recommended Actions for Usability Specialists
- Because developing usable software is not the sole responsibility of only one party, usability specialists should encourage all project team members to take responsibility for the process.
- Usability specialists should allocate more time for consulting with end users and should bypass proxies such as user representatives or business units.
- Usability specialists should conduct user research.
- While conducting user research, usability specialists should identify the usage patterns of users.

- Usability specialists should listen to, observe, and try to understand users and their needs.
- Usability specialists should begin usability testing as early as possible by using prototypes.

As mentioned in the recommended actions, regardless of the position one holds in a company, business units and project team members can have a profound effect on contributing to an IT project's success by making small changes in their work practices. With the right amount of will and determination, such adjustments can be easily achieved.

Index

Human resource management, 31

I
Impact, 62, 63, 64, 65, 144, 149
Impact analysis, 39
In-scope, 35
Information architecture, 98, 110, 120, 121
Information Technology Infrastructure Library (ITIL®), 46, 47
Integration management, 31
Integration test, 134
Interaction design, 98, 107, 110, 114, 115, 120, 121
Interface design, 108, 110, 114, 115, 120, 121, 122
International Software Testing Qualifications Board (ISTQB®), 61, 73, 79, 83, 111
Interview, 6, 37, 63, 115, 116

K
Keyword-driven test automation, 87, 92

L
Low-fidelity prototype, 121

M
Maintainable test scripts, 92
Maturity of the system under test (SUT), 87, 88
Method, 27
Mind mapping, 121
Module, 134
Moscow prioritization technique, 38
Must-have need, 144

N
Navigation design, 110, 120, 121
Need to change, 43
Nice-to-have need, 91, 113, 144
Non-functional requirement, 3, 9, 10, 11, 12, 20, 21, 36, 61, 77, 97, 101, 102, 144, 145, 149, 150
Non-functional test, 136
Not able, 44
Not knowing, 43
Not willing, 44, 45, 46

O

Object, 23, 27, 28, 29, 30
Object-oriented approach, 21, 23, 24, 25, 27, 28, 29, 30, 145
Objective, 3, 5, 6, 10, 11, 12, 18, 20, 34, 35, 37, 38, 39, 61, 122
Operational level agreement (OLA), 46, 47
Out-of-scope, 34, 35, 38
Out-of-scope change request/demand, 34, 38

P

Paper prototype, 121
Partition, 72, 73, 74
Performance, 9, 20, 61, 97, 101, 102, 136, 137, 145
Persona, 110, 111, 115, 116, 124, 125, 129
Persona identification, 110
Primary scenario, 9, 110
Priority, 64, 65
Probability, 62, 63, 65, 66
Procedure, 27
Process flow, 11, 29, 30, 36, 114, 115
Process flow design, 114
Procurement management, 31
Project, 6, 10, 33
Project goal, 17, 20, 41, 148
Project management, 31, 33, 34, 145
Project Management Body of Knowledge (PMBOK®), 31, 33, 38, 61
Project Management Institute (PMI), 31, 33, 34
Project management knowledge areas, 31, 33, 34
Project manager, 47, 111, 141, 146, 151
Project objective, 35, 38, 61
Project stakeholder, 36, 144, 151
Proof of concept (POC), 92
Prototyping, 110, 112, 122
Pseudocode, 55, 77, 78, 80

Q

Quality management, 31
Quick-win, 45, 47

R

RACI matrix, 126
Radar chart, 38

156

System test, 134, 135

T
Task analysis, 121
Technical test analyst, 55, 56, 83
Test analyst, 55, 56, 83
Test automation, 85, 87, 88, 89, 90, 91, 92, 151
Test basis, 77
Test case, 37, 38, 55, 70, 71, 72, 73, 74, 75, 77, 78, 79, 80, 81, 82, 83,
        85, 87, 91, 92, 135, 136, 137, 146, 149, 151
Test case naming/numbering, 92
Test design technique, 51, 56, 57, 62, 63, 66, 67, 69, 70, 74
Test effort estimation, 66
Test execution frequency, 87, 88, 89, 90, 91
Test level, 133, 134, 135, 137
Test type, 133, 135, 137
Testing effectiveness, 85
Testing efficiency, 85, 92
Testing organization and skills, 51, 55, 57
Testing processes, 51, 54, 57
Testing terminology and culture of quality, 51, 53, 54, 57
Testing tools, 51, 57, 92, 146, 151
Thinking aloud, 121
Time management, 31, 146
Traceability matrix, 38, 39, 88, 144
Tree testing, 121

U
Uncategorized requirement, 35
Unclear requirement, 37
Unit test, 53, 134, 145
Usability, 9, 20, 55, 61, 93, 95, 97, 98, 99, 100, 101, 102, 103, 105,
        107, 108, 109, 111, 112, 113, 115, 117, 119, 120, 122, 123,
        125, 126, 127, 128, 129, 130, 136, 145
Usability processes, 107, 109, 112, 113, 115, 147
Usability specialist, 100, 101, 1107, 108, 111, 117, 125, 126, 127,
        129, 141, 147, 151, 152
Usability testing, 107, 110, 111, 112, 119, 128, 129, 131, 133, 147,
        152
Usage pattern tracking, 121
Use case, 7, 23, 24, 29, 55, 63, 135

158